THE
ADVOCATE
&
THE
ADVERSARY

JACK REHILL

Copyright

© 2023 Jack Rehill
© 2023 Cover Design by Mason B. Wooldridge
Interior Design by Amit Dey

Published in the United States of America
All rights reserved worldwide
Authentic Endeavors Publishing/
Kingdom Book Endeavors

No part of this book may be reproduced by any mechanical, photographic, or electronic process, or in any form of audio or digital recording, nor may it be stored in any retrieval system, transmitted or otherwise, be copied for public or private use – other than for fair use as a brief quotation embodied in articles and review without prior written permission of the author, illustrators or publisher.

ISBN: 978-1-955668-66-8 (Paperback)
ISBN: 978-1-955668-67-5 (eBook)

LCCN 2023914268

Dedication

This book is dedicated to the memory of our
firstborn, beloved son, Jeffrey,
who is now and forever
in the presence of our most precious
Lord and Savior, Jesus Christ.

*Trust in the Lord with all your heart and lean
not on your own understanding.
In all your ways acknowledge Him, and
He shall direct your paths*
Proverbs 3:5-6

Acknowledgments

First and foremost, I am most grateful for the love of my life, Patricia, who has stood with me through thick and thin, battles without, and battles within, these past 51 years. She has never wavered in her loyalty, faithfulness and love for the truth in Christ Jesus.

I am so grateful that the Lord blessed us with three other children, Joshua, Jared, and Johanna, as well as a daughter-in-law Kara, and son-in-law Mason, and two precious granddaughters, Lyla and Claudia.

I would like to also acknowledge George Veach who was a faithful spiritual father and mentor to us throughout most of our Christian lives, who also now and forever stands in the glorious presence of our Lord and Savior Jesus Christ.

Table of Contents

Dedication iii
Acknowledgments v
Introduction ix
Chapter 1:   The Rear Attack 1
Chapter 2:   The Frontal Attack 21
Chapter 3:   The Glory and the Story 53
Chapter 4:   Moses: Let My People Go 85
Chapter 5:   David – A Man After God's Own Heart . . . 117
Chapter 6:   The Lord Jesus Christ – The Advocate . . . 143
About the Author 169

Introduction

I have encountered too many people who, after putting their faith in Christ, have become disillusioned and discouraged, and begin to question their faith. Some give up their walk with the Lord when troubles, trials, and tragedies come into their lives because they were under the impression that their faith would exempt them from all such things. They abandon their faith in Christ simply because of ignorance.

In Second Corinthians 2:11, Paul says, "Lest Satan should take advantage of us; for we are not ignorant of his devices." We should not be ignorant regarding how Satan works. If we are ignorant of his devices, we will be deceived, taken advantage of, and ultimately defeated. Hosea 4:6 says in part, "My people are destroyed for lack of knowledge." This is not God's plan for us. We will have conflict, but conflict doesn't have to have us. If we have the knowledge of God and His Word, we will come to understand that we are only the subjects of a greater conflict between our Advocate and our adversary. The conflict will eventually give way to conquest by the hand of our Conqueror and Advocate, the Lord

Jesus Christ. If you are a true believer in Christ and love God and His will, it should not surprise you that you have an Advocate and an adversary. We have One who is for us, and we have one who is against us.

The moment we pledge our allegiance to our Advocate, the battle lines are drawn. Our adversary is enraged that he no longer has power over us, and he is determined to destroy us. First Peter 5:8 warns us to "be sober [self-controlled], be vigilant [watchful]; because your adversary the devil walks about like a roaring lion, seeking whom he may devour." The apostle Peter is speaking to believers here; be on your guard, don't be caught off guard. You have an adversary who is seeking to devour you. This is not something we should necessarily be fearful of, but mindful of. This is really the point of this book.

An advocate actively favors or fights for one who meets opposition. In John 14:16, Jesus tells His disciples that He's going to send another Helper to them after He ascends back into heaven and sits at the right hand of the throne of God. The Greek word for *helper* in this verse is *parakletos* (par-ak'-lay-tos) which can also be translated *advocate*.[1] Jesus is saying in effect, "I have been your Advocate, and now I am going to send you another Advocate, One beside Me, but one just like Me because He will testify of Me" (John 15:26, author's paraphrase).

---

[1] Strong, James. "3875 παράκλητος (parakletos)," Strong's Greek: 3875. παράκλητος (parakletos) (BibleHub, 2023), https://biblehub.com/greek/strongs/3875.htm.

In a court of law, an advocate refers to a person who is qualified to plead the case of another. There was no one more qualified to plead our case than the Lord Jesus. He was willing to pay the penalty for our sin. His death—in place of ours—broke the power of sin over us with His resurrection. He sent the power of His life, the Holy Spirit, to us with His ascension. He was the only qualified person on earth, because only a sinless sacrifice could save us. And no one else would lay down their life for a friend, let alone their enemies. Only the sinless Son of God would do that, "for scarcely for a righteous man will one die; yet perhaps for a good man someone would even dare to die. But God demonstrates His own love toward us, in that while we were still sinners [enemies of God], Christ died for us" (Rom. 5:7–8).

The Advocate and the adversary

An adversary is an opponent, one who contends with, opposes, or resists another. The Hebrew word for *adversary* is *satan*, meaning accuser, one who obstructs, or opposes.[2] An advocate is for us; an adversary is against us.

The good news is that if God, our Advocate, is for us, who, men or devils, can be against us (Rom. 8:31)? God was for us even before we were for Him. How much more will He be for those that are now for Him, whose lives are given over to Him? However, what we as Christians may fail to understand is that the more we are for our Advocate,

---

[2] Strong, James. "7854 שָׂטָן (satan)," Strong's Hebrew: 7854. שָׂטָן (satan) (BibleHub, 2023), https://biblehub.com/hebrew/7854.htm.

the more our adversary is against us. The Lord Jesus says in Luke 10:19, "Behold, I give you the authority to trample on serpents and scorpions, and over all the power of the enemy, and nothing shall by any means hurt you." We must understand that we are in a war between light and darkness, between the armies of the Lord of hosts and the hordes of hell. The advantage we have as Christians is the knowledge that we have the victory through our Lord Jesus Christ and the power of the Holy Spirit. However, it is still a fight, and it is a fight to the finish.

Our Advocate has given us the promise of authority over the enemy, but that is only realized by our willingness to engage in the battle. God told Moses to tell the people to go in and take the land, for He had already given it to them. However, they would never possess the land that God had already promised was theirs unless they were willing to go in and take it, which meant having to face the giants that occupied the land. This was something they weren't willing to do at that time. Why would God give them a land that was filled with giants bigger and more powerful than them? To prove that He was able to do what He said, and also to prove their faith in Him.

Before the apostle Paul left this earth, under the inspiration of the Holy Spirit, he said in writing to his spiritual son Timothy, "I have fought the good fight, I have finished the race, I have kept the faith" (2 Tim. 4:7). He previously wrote to Timothy, "Fight the good fight of faith, lay hold on eternal life" (1 Tim. 6:12). We have eternal life through our advocate the Lord Jesus Christ, but we must lay hold of it. We must take it to receive it, and we have an adversary who is going to do everything he can to keep us from taking it. And so, we fight, "not as one who beats the air," as the apostle Paul says in First Corinthians 9:26, but as verse 27 says, as one who disciplines our body and brings it into subjection to God and leaves no room for our adversary to gain an advantage through the weakness of the flesh.

In Second Timothy 2:3, the apostle Paul again speaks to Timothy, saying, "You therefore must endure hardship as a good soldier of Jesus Christ." A soldier suggests an army, and an army suggests war.

Chapter One

The Rear Attack

> *So, God created man in His own image; in the image of God, He created them; male and female He created them. Then God blessed them, and God said to them, "Be fruitful and multiply; fill the earth and subdue it; have dominion over the fish of the sea, over the birds of the air, and over every living thing that moves on the earth." And God said, "See, I have given you every herb that yields seed which is on the face of all the earth, and every tree whose fruit yields seed; to you it shall be for food." (Gen. 1:27–29)*

God created man and woman in His own image. The Advocate bestowed such favor on man and woman that they bore His own glorious image, which meant that they were to be as He was upon the earth. First John 4:17 tells us, "As He is, so are we in this world." They were His delegates with His fruitfulness, His authority, and His provision.

The woman would have no pain in childbirth. The man would not have to work by the sweat of his brow for his food. They would have authority over every living thing that moved upon the face of the earth. There would be perfect order and peace upon the earth by the hand of the Advocate.

> *The Lord God planted a garden eastward in Eden, and there He put the man whom He had formed. And out of the ground the Lord God made every tree grow that is pleasant to the sight and good for food. The tree of life was also in the midst of the garden, and the tree of the knowledge of good and evil. Now a river went out of Eden to water the garden, and from there it parted and became four riverheads. (Gen. 2:8-10)*

If that wasn't enough, God planted a garden where He placed the man. The man would not have to plant it; the Advocate planted it and supplied it with every tree that is pleasant to the sight and good for food—good food! But more than that, God created out of the body of the man a helper comparable to him, a companion with whom to share in all that the Advocate provided. And the grand finale was the Advocate's intent to live in the garden with both of them forever. They would know the inexpressible, unsurpassed, unbroken, never-ending joy of His presence! It doesn't get any better than that.

Now comes the rear attack of the adversary. God had commanded the man not to eat from the tree of the knowledge of good and evil. The Scriptures don't tell us that God warned the man that there would be a snake lurking in the garden who would try to tempt them into disobeying the command of God. First of all, why would God allow there to be a snake in the garden? Secondly, why would He not warn them that that snake was there? We must remember that God made mankind with one ability that all of the rest of His creation did not possess—the power to choose. God intentionally made humans in His own likeness and image. He desired to have a relationship with them based on willful love and trust, not a forced relationship based on coercion. God wanted us to willfully choose Him as He had willfully chosen us. If He had warned them about the snake, how could their love for Him, and their trust in Him be proven? We have all experienced situations, troubles, and tragedies that God did not warn us about in advance, except to let us know generally, as the Lord Jesus said in John 16:33 that we would experience these things in this world. Our relationship with Him is based on faith, trust, and love. We have faith in His goodness and trust in His judgment. We believe in His unfailing love for us and ours for Him.

Genesis 3:1 says, "Now the serpent was more cunning than any beast of the field."

The word *cunning* here means shrewd, crafty, sly; one who is seeking to gain advantage over another for their own selfish interests.[3]

---

[3] Strong, James. "6175 עָרוּם (arum)," Strong's Hebrew: 6175. עָרוּם (arum) (BibleHub, 2023), https://biblehub.com/hebrew/6175.htm.

Second Corinthians 11:14 says that Satan (our adversary) transforms himself into an angel of light. In other words, he makes himself out to be an agent of God to enlighten us. The adversary appears to be our advocate, contending for us, when in reality he is dead set against us. However, if we have the knowledge of God through His Word, we understand that our adversary will always try to get in the back door. He uses our flesh with its desires and appetites. He wants us to act according to our will, not the will of God, as we shall see.

Let's look at what we will call the four Ds: Doubt which leads to Deception, which brings about Disobedience, which brings Destruction.

The adversary starts his rear attack by beginning to sow seeds of doubt into our minds regarding the Word of God. Has God indeed said? Are you sure about that? Is that what He really meant? Also, notice the spin the adversary puts on the question in Genesis 3:1: "Has God indeed said, 'You shall not eat of every tree of the garden?'" You mean there's a tree that you can't eat from? Why would there be a tree you couldn't eat from? Did God really say that?

Eve did not realize that the serpent was deliberately drawing her attention away from the rest of the trees of the garden, which God gave her to eat from, and toward the one tree he knew would kill her and rob her of the God-given authority she had over the earth. That's what he was after— the dominion God had given to her and Adam. He wanted to steal it from them so he could become the "prince of the power of the air" (Eph. 2:2).

The Lord Jesus says in John 10:10 that "the thief [Satan] does not come except to steal, and to kill, and to destroy." He doesn't come for any other reason. He never comes with good intentions. He never comes for our benefit, only for his. He is our adversary and always will be until he is cast into the lake of fire.

Now Eve attempts to respond, but she is no match for her adversary, and neither are we. He is too shrewd and cunning for us. As soon as the first seed of doubt is suggested, we should immediately recognize the source. God would never introduce doubt toward what He said in His Word, even when it appears that He is keeping something good from us. That was exactly the strategy of the serpent—the rear attack.

Why would God keep something good from you and threaten you with death? If He is really a good God, He wouldn't do that to you. He just doesn't want you to be on the same level as Him and know what he knows. He wants to keep you in the dark, and keep you down. Can you really trust a God like that? He's not really for you. You don't have to listen to Him. You can be your own god.

This is the rear attack. Satan lies to us, pretending to be our advocate, in order to steal us away from our true Advocate.

The serpent adversary steps up the rear attack upon Eve with deception veiled in two final statements: "You will not surely die," and "God knows that in the day you eat of it your eyes will be opened, and you will be like God, knowing good and evil" (Gen. 3:4–5). Again, the adversary deceives

Eve into thinking that being like God and knowing good and evil would be a good thing. In reality, it would kill her and Adam and bring death upon everything that God created.

This second D after doubt is deception which is probably the most deadly, because it seduces us into believing the lie that leads to disobedience, and ultimately, destruction. So, as soon as doubts come into our mind about God and His Word, we need to recognize the source. God is not the source of doubt. He is the source of faith. When doubts come, immediately cast them down, taking them captive to the obedience of the Lord Jesus Christ (2 Cor. 10:5).

Eve lingered, and allowed the adversary to continue the dialogue, instead of ending it and getting out of there.

The serpent, appealing to, as First John 2:16 says, "the lust of the flesh, the lust of the eyes, and the pride of life," succeeded in weakening Eve's ability to resist the temptation.

> So, when the woman saw that the tree was good for food [the lust of the flesh], that it was pleasant to the eyes [the lust of the eyes], and a tree desirable to make one wise [the pride of life], she took of its fruit and ate. She also gave to her husband with her, and he ate. (Gen. 3:6)

Eve disobeyed the command of God not to eat from the tree of the knowledge of good and evil. Not only did she disobey, but she "gave to her husband with her and he ate" and he disobeyed. Our disobedience not only has dire consequences for us personally, but can also take others down with us. This is now the third D, disobedience. The serpent had accomplished his goal, to steal, kill, and ultimately destroy, bringing about the fourth D, destruction. We don't see the rear attack coming because it looks so good, seems so right, and makes sense to our finite minds. However, as Proverbs 14:12 says, "There is a way that seems right to a man, But its end is the way of death." The spiritual person does not live according to the will of the flesh, but according to the will of the Spirit which is always in agreement with the will of the Father. Therefore, whatever appeals to my flesh, whatever appeals to my eyes, and whatever appeals to my pride is not of the Father. This should serve as a warning to me that my adversary is engaging in the rear attack to get me off track.

The adversary employed the same strategy with the last Adam, the Lord Jesus, in the wilderness. However, the last Adam would not fail the test as the first Adam did. There would never be a need for another Adam— hence, the designation of the "last Adam" to refer to the Lord Jesus.

This last Adam was tested far more severely than the first Adam. Luke 4:1–14 describes it in detail. First of all, we see that the Lord Jesus, being filled with the Holy Spirit, was led by the spirit into the wilderness to be tested by the devil. Why would the Spirit lead the Lord Jesus into a wilderness, which in the Greek[4] means a solitary, lonely, desolate place with no resources available, to be tested by the devil?

---

[4] Strong, James. "2048 ἔρημος (erémos)," Strong's Greek: 2048. ἔρημος (erémos) (BibleHub, 2023), https://biblehub.com/greek/strongs/2048.htm.

Because there is an adversary in this world who is going to test us, and we must be filled with the power of the Holy Spirit to pass the test. How often have we found ourselves in the wilderness, being harassed by the adversary in one way or another right after a high point in our journey with the Lord? The great preacher Charles Spurgeon, after preaching to thousands on a Sunday morning, and seeing hundreds saved by the grace of God, would often, by Tuesday, have to call for the elders of the church to pray for him because he was in the wilderness being battered with depression.

First John 3:8 says that the Lord Jesus was manifested, or came into this world, to destroy the works of the devil. He couldn't destroy the works of the devil without dealing with the devil, and he couldn't be shown or proven to be the Son of God without defeating the devil as only the Son of God could do, being filled with the Spirit. He has gone before us with His death on the cross to gain the victory for us. He rose from the grave and ascended back to the Father so that He could send the same Spirit that lived in Him to live victoriously in us. However, living victoriously won't be without a wilderness, and overcoming our adversary won't be without a battle. There is no victory without a battle.

I believe that every true Christian will have wilderness experiences. They will be tested by our adversary to prove that they belong to the Son of God and to bring us to a total dependence upon and faith in the Son of God. Furthermore, I believe that this is the process by which we are made partakers of His authority. We might speak with His authority and walk and act with the power of His authority when we have been completely brought under His authority. There is no easy way around it. There are no shortcuts. We must have a willingness to take up our cross and be crucified with Christ, that we might be raised with Him and reign together with Him by the power of His authority.

First John 5:4–5 says, "For whatever is born of God overcomes the world. And this is the victory that has overcome the world [and the prince of this world]—our faith. Who is he who overcomes the world [and the prince of this world], but he who believes that Jesus is the Son of God?" It's one thing to "know" that Jesus is the son of God, but it's another thing to "believe" it. God's plan is to make believers out of us—believers who overcome by the same Spirit and authority as our Advocate.

> *Then some of the itinerant Jewish exorcists took it upon themselves to call the name of the Lord Jesus over those who had evil spirits, saying, "We exorcise you by the Jesus whom Paul preaches." Also, there were seven sons of Sceva, a Jewish chief priest, who did so. And the evil spirit answered and said, "Jesus I know, and Paul I know; but who are you?"*
>
> (Acts 19:13–15)

Notice that it says they "took it upon themselves" to call upon the name of the Lord Jesus. They did not know the One whose name they were proclaiming. They took it upon themselves. They were not in submission and under the authority of the name that they were proclaiming. They took it upon themselves, and therefore, they were not recognized as having any authority to speak in the name of One they did not know, Jesus. You cannot fool the adversary and his hordes; they know the authentic from the imitators, and they have no fear of imitators who have no authority.

An imitation doesn't have the same quality as the real thing. These imitators had not been tried, tested, proven, and authorized to speak or command with any authority in the name of the Lord Jesus. The evil spirit within this man knew it. Our adversary knows who possesses the authority of the Lord Jesus and can recognize imitators.

Our adversary says, "Jesus I know. I incited the crowd to kill Him even when Pilate wanted to release Him, but He rose from the dead and stripped me of my authority. Now I tremble in His presence and flee from Him. Paul I know. I was permitted to incite the authorities to imprison him frequently, confront him with death often, beat him five times with thirty-nine stripes, three times with rods, stone him to death once, but he was raised up. He was shipwrecked three times, spent a night and a day in the deep. He was in journeys often, and perils of waters, and perils of robbers, and perils of his own countrymen, and perils of the Gentiles, and perils of the city, and perils of the wilderness, in perils of the sea, in perils among false brethren; in weariness and toil, and sleepless nights often, and hunger and thirst, often without food, and in cold and nakedness" (2 Cor. 11:23-27, author's paraphrase). In spite of all this, Paul was able to say that none of those things moved him from faith in the Lord Jesus, and he finished his race with joy (Acts 20:24). We cannot speak or act with any authority unless we have been there, unless we've been tried, tested, and proven to be His. Our adversary knows who we are and who we are not. "Jesus, I know, Paul I know, but who are you?" It really begs the question: Who am I in Christ? Am I in Christ? Is He in me? How well do I know Him, and how well does He know me?

An authorized representative of any company does not represent their own interests, but the interests of the company they represent. To ensure this is so, they must go through strict, prescribed training that indoctrinates them with the core values of the company. When the company is satisfied that their interests have become the interests of the representative, they will be duly authorized with the full authority and backing of the company they represent. They will have the power to speak and act on the company's behalf. Our heavenly Father has a training program individually designed to rid us of all self-interest and bring us into complete and total dependence upon the Holy Spirit and submission to His authority. When we are willing to submit ourselves to His program, then we will have His authority and full backing to speak and act on His behalf, according to His will in the name of Jesus. Our adversary will know it and know us.

The man and woman fell prey to the working principle of their adversary, rebelling against God, taking matters into their own hands, and declaring their independence from God. As a result, they put themselves under the power of their adversary. Their Advocate could no longer be for them because of their disobedience. He was no longer working or walking with them; they were on their own, driven out of the garden of His presence.

Now, the woman will have pain in childbirth (Gen. 3:16); now, the man will work by the sweat of his brow (v. 19) all because he listened to the voice of his wife (v. 17), who had listened to the voice of the adversary. It is critical to know the voice of our Advocate, and to be able to distinguish it from every other voice. The Lord Jesus gave us a clue about how we can make that distinction in Matthew 16:21–23, where He tells His disciples that He is going to suffer and be killed at the hands of the religious leaders and be raised up on the third day. Upon hearing this, Peter began to rebuke Him, saying that this would never happen to Him. Jesus's response to Peter was very strong. In fact, it was not to Peter, but to the adversary who, unbeknown to Peter, was speaking through him. "Get behind Me Satan! You are an offense to Me, for you are not mindful of the things of God, but the things of men." Our adversary will always appeal to our flesh and human interests, rather than to the Spirit and God's interests.

"Then the Lord called to Adam and said to him, 'Where are you?'" (Gen. 3:9) The voice of our Advocate will always call us to account for acting contrary to His commands. He wants to bring our actions to light to be judged and corrected. On the other hand, our adversary, who is also referred to as "the accuser of our brethren" (Rev. 12:10), will do just that when we fall short of God's commands. "Now you've done it, and you call yourself a Christian? Who do you think you're kidding? God knows you're a hypocrite and has no use for you." Our Advocate will always convict and correct to bring us back to Him; our adversary will accuse and condemn to drive us further from Him.

Another strategy our adversary may employ in keeping with his nature as the prince of darkness, is to suggest that we continue to hide our wrongdoing and ignore the convicting power of the Holy Spirit. In effect, this keeps us under the power of the darkness that is in opposition to the light. The darkness blinds us to the truth of the light of God's Word which leads to eternal life. If I refuse to come into the light, eventually I will be cast into outer, eternal darkness, which God is not willing that anyone should suffer. Those who have overcome an addiction to drugs, alcohol, or any other life-controlling behavior know that the first step to recovery was confession—coming into the light, admitting the truth about themselves and their need for help. When I don't do that, and I continue to hide the truth, I am bound by the power of darkness. I am not set free. I am bound by anxiety, worry, and fear. The path to freedom is to come into the light of truth.

The apostle Paul, writing to the church at Thessalonica says that we are children of the light. We are not of the night or of darkness. (1Thess. 5:5)

In Genesis 3:11, God asks the man, "Who told you that you were naked?"

The voice of our adversary can come into our thoughts by way of suggestions, doubts, worry, or fear. It can come through the mouths of others. It can even come through well-meaning friends and family, those closest to us. In Genesis 3:17, God says to Adam, "because you have heeded the voice of your wife." Those closest to us can be used by our adversary to lead us away from the will and command of God without realizing it, thinking that they are looking out for us. As mentioned previously, this was the case with Peter when the Lord Jesus spoke of His impending death. Peter was saying, "We've left everything to follow You. We love You. You are the Christ, the Son of the living God, and now You're telling us You're leaving? We don't want a dead Messiah; we want You to overthrow the Roman government and set up Your kingdom right here and right now so we can rule with You. We're going to fight for it with You, and even die for it with You if need be." Peter still didn't understand that His kingdom had to first be established internally. In order for that to happen, the Lord Jesus had to give His life, for His life was the life of the kingdom, and that life is marked by "righteousness and peace and joy in the Holy Spirit" (Rom. 14:17).

It would have been quite tempting to listen to such an impassioned statement from such a close friend; it sounded so right. However, the Lord Jesus had a closer Friend than that, and that was His Father whose voice was the only voice He listened to. He didn't hear that voice coming from His close friend Peter. He heard another voice, the voice of His foe and not His Father, appealing to His flesh to keep Him from doing the will of the One Who sent Him to the earth, and He called it out, "Get behind Me, Satan. Get out of My way."

> *While He was still talking to the multitudes, behold, His mother and brothers stood outside, seeking to speak with Him. [Why weren't they inside listening to Him, rather than outside wanting Him to come out and listen to them?] Then one said to Him, "Look, Your mother and Your brothers are standing outside, seeking to speak with You." But He answered and said to the one who told Him, "Who is My mother and who are My brothers?"*
>
> (Matt. 12:46–48)

Didn't the Lord Jesus know who His mother was and who His brothers were? Of course He did, but that is not how He defined family. "And He stretched out His hand toward His disciples and said, 'Here are my mother and my brothers! For whoever does the will of my Father in heaven is my brother and sister and mother'" (Matt. 12:49-50). Again, the Lord Jesus makes the distinction between flesh and spirit by essentially saying, "My true relatives are those who have the same Father I do, and they show themselves to be so by doing His will as I do."

In the world we live in today, we see the celebration and even deification of the carnal nature of mankind. It's all about whatever pleases us, whatever makes us feel good, which is completely the opposite of the Kingdom of God. This worldview is perpetuated by the prince of this world, the ruler of this world, the adversary. God never meant for the adversary to be the ruler of this world. He meant for the man, together with his wife, and the rest of mankind to have dominion over this world under His rule. He meant for His Kingdom to be on earth "as it is in heaven" (Matt. 6:10). In other words, heaven on earth.

Furthermore, He intended for the adversary to be under the rule of mankind as long as they remained under the rule of God. In fact, that is what the Kingdom of God is: a God-ruled people. However, as we know, the man and the woman gave in to the trickery of the adversary and, in essence, declared their independence from the rule of God, believing they could rule themselves. The man and the woman did not create themselves, and they were not created to rule themselves. They didn't have the capacity to rule themselves. They were created to be dependent upon God. They were not created to be independent. They were created to live forever with God upon the earth He created in everlasting love, joy, and peace. They were not created to live forever apart from God in the lake of fire reserved for the adversary and his captives in everlasting torment. They were created to be led by that Great Shepherd of the sheep, the Lord Jesus, Who said in John 10:27,

"My sheep hear [or listen to] My voice, and I know them, and they follow Me."

Psalm 100:3 says, "Know that the Lord, He is God; It is He Who has made us, and not we ourselves; We are His people and the sheep of His pasture." We have heard some proudly declare that they are self-made men or women when, in fact, they couldn't even keep breathing if God did not keep their lungs working. Our lives in this fallen world are so fragile. At any given moment, they can be snuffed out. James 4:14 says, "you do not know what will happen tomorrow. For what is your life? It is even a vapor that appears for a little time and then vanishes away." We were made to be led, not to lead ourselves.

Society has thousands of books and seminars on leadership. We have world leaders. We were created to be led. We have leaders and followers in this world. Most of us are followers, but even leaders were followers before they became leaders. Who is leading the leaders? Whose voice are they listening to? The adversary knew the man and the woman were created to be led. So, he sought to lead them astray, out from under the rule of God and under his rule.

Years ago, Bob Dylan wrote a song entitled, "Gotta Serve Somebody." He sang about choosing to serve either God or Satan. There are only two true sources of leadership: the Advocate or the adversary. All of mankind will serve one of them, because we were made that way.

Earlier, we asked the question, Why did God allow the serpent into the garden of Eden? It might be more accurate to ask, Why did God permit the serpent to remain there? I believe he was already there before the man and woman were put there. "You were in Eden, the garden of God; ... The workmanship of your timbrels and pipes was prepared for you on the day you were created" (Ezek. 28:13). This verse is speaking of the rise and fall of the King of Tyre, but many believe it is also speaking of the rise and fall of Lucifer. He was created with beautiful attributes to be with God in the garden of His presence until "iniquity was found in [him]" (v.15), the source of which was pride. He was then cast out of heaven and down to the ground, suggesting he was no longer in fellowship with God. He was now an enemy of God. He became the adversary, but still remained in Eden.

Second Corinthians 6:14–15 says in part, "What communion has light with darkness? And what accord has Christ [our Advocate] with Belial [our adversary]?" None! I believe God left the serpent in the garden to test the man and his wife, whether they would follow His command and His leading. Whose voice would they listen to? I also believe God left the serpent there to bring him under the dominion of the man and the woman.

Genesis 3:1 says, "Now the serpent was more cunning than any beast of the field which the Lord God had made." The serpent was a beast of the field inhabited by Satan himself, who had the ability to speak through the serpent. God gave the man and woman dominion over every living thing that moves upon the earth which included the serpent

(Gen. 1:28). The Hebrew word for dominion is radah (raw-daw). It means to rule, to tread down, to subjugate, to reign, and to prevail against.[5]

Right from the beginning, mankind had an Advocate and an adversary. However, as long as the man and woman listened to their Advocate, and were willing to follow His lead, they would rule over their adversary. He would not rule over them if they remained under the rule of God. The adversary might come against them, but he couldn't have them. Ultimately, they would prevail against him by the power of their Advocate because of their obedience to their Advocate. This is true in our own lives if we have surrendered to the rule and Lordship of Jesus Christ.

The Lord Jesus said to his followers in Luke 10:18–19, "I saw Satan fall like lightning from heaven. Behold, I give you the authority to trample on serpents and scorpions, and over all the power of the enemy, and nothing shall by any means hurt you." Again, the enemy may have at me, but he cannot have me. He cannot hurt me in the sense of snatching me out of the hand, and out from under the grace, of my Advocate.

In Romans 16:20, the apostle Paul says, "The God of peace will crush Satan [your adversary] under your feet shortly." Who is the God of peace? None other than the Lord Jesus Christ, who is our peace, the One who came to destroy the works of the devil. The One under whom all

---

[5] Strong, James. "7287 הָדָר (radah)," Strong's Hebrew: 7287. הָדָר (radah) (BibleHub, 2023), https://biblehub.com/hebrew/7287.htm.

authority in heaven and earth has been given to restore to us the authority and power over our adversary that had been lost in the garden.

In Matthew 16:18, the Lord Jesus says, "On this rock [speaking of Peter] I will build My church, and the gates of Hades shall not prevail against it." The Lord Jesus, the Advocate, came to set the captives free, those bound by the adversary, and build them into a body of believers and receivers of His light and life and love under His authority. The gates of hell will not prevail, but they would assail. They prevailed against the first Adam and his wife and those who came after them, but they will not prevail against this last Adam, the head of His church, the Lord Jesus Christ.

Chapter Two

The Frontal Attack

The Lord Jesus promised us that the gates of hell would not prevail against us. However, we must come to grips with the fact that the war wages on. The issue becomes, Are we willing to endure to the end? It's not only a matter of starting, but how and whether we finish. Am I still believing at the end as I did at the beginning? The apostle Paul said right before his death, "I have fought the good fight, I have finished the race, I have kept the faith" (2 Tim. 4:7). In Luke 18:8, the Lord Jesus asks, "When the Son of Man comes, will He really find faith on the earth?" This refers to the end when He returns. In Matthew 24:13, Jesus says, when speaking of the events that will occur before the end, "He who endures to the end shall be saved."

The war wages on as depicted in Revelation 12:13–17, where the adversary is characterized by a dragon who is persecuting the church. However, she (the church) is given two wings of a great eagle to fly away from the adversary for a time to be kept from his presence. The adversary spews out a flood against her to sweep her away, but the earth opens and swallows up the flood. It is comforting to know that our God is the one who determines the battle schedule. Our God is the one who determines the times and seasons. Our God is the one who determines when we fight and when we rest from the battle, all while building up our most holy faith in our most holy God.

In verse 17, the dragon is enraged with the church and goes out to make war with the rest of her offspring, those "who keep the commandments of God and have the testimony of Jesus Christ." These are the ones who have the life of the Lord Jesus reproduced in them and coming forth from them as witnesses. They keep His commandments and have His testimony, and only do what they see Him doing. It's not just a matter of knowing God's commands, Word, or will, it is believing in them that moves me to keep them and do them.

First John 2:4 says, "He who says, 'I know Him,' and does not keep His commandments, is a liar, and the truth is not in him." Our adversary knows who the liars are; it takes one to know one. They are no threat to his kingdom. However, he is enraged with those who believe and keep the commandments of God and makes war with them. If that's you, don't be surprised. As First Peter 4:12 says, don't think that it is some strange thing happening to you. It's not strange at all; it has been so from the beginning. We have an Advocate, and those who belong to Him and keep His commandments have an angry adversary. If the adversary cannot succeed with the rear attack, to deceive us into disobeying the commands of God and losing the testimony of the Lord Jesus Christ, he becomes enraged and engages us with a frontal attack.

Acts 14:22 says that through many tribulations we enter the kingdom of God. The Lord Jesus forewarned us in John 16:33 that in the world we would have trouble, and that's because the prince of this world, our adversary, is a troublemaker. You can't live in a troubled world and not have trouble. However, the Lord Jesus goes on to say, "But be of good cheer, I [your Advocate] have overcome the world." He overcame every trouble we would ever have, all our tribulation. He overcame sin, death, and the grave by the power of the Holy Spirit. He sent that same spirit to live and breathe and empower us to do likewise.

Matthew 11:12 says that "from the days of John the Baptist until now the kingdom of heaven suffers violence, and the violent take it by force." That force is with us, and in us, and for us. Our Advocate is not an imaginary, nameless "Force," but the third Person of the Trinity, the blessed Holy Spirit. The word violence in the Greek is biazó (bee-ad'-zo). It means to use force, to be pressed or seized.[6] Our adversary will attempt to apply force or pressure upon us with negative circumstances, negative outcomes, and negative thinking. He might say, for example, "You are not going to make it. This isn't going to work out. God doesn't really care about you. If He did, this would not have happened."

---

[6] Strong, James. "971 βιάζομαι (biazó)," Strong's Greek: 971. βιάζομαι (biazó) (BibleHub, 2023), https://biblehub.com/greek/strongs/971.htm.

Our adversary will always try to get us to think the worst. He will attempt to seize us with worry and fear and anxiety to the point where we cannot move. But the violent move, the violent press on believing God. Another Greek word for violent is biastés (bee-as-tace'). This word means strong, forceful, and energetic.[7] The power of the Holy Spirit in us is greater, stronger, more forceful, and more powerful than our adversary against us.

Romans 8:31 says in part, "If God is for us, who can be against us?" Our adversary can be against us, but he cannot prevail over us, because our Advocate has already prevailed over him through the cross.

There are four words in the Greek for power. The primary one that is most widely used is dunamis (doo'-nam-is).[8] It means energy, might, great force, great strength. This power overcomes all resistance. Dunamis is where we get the word dynamite, suggesting the explosive power of our Advocate within us to blow up and blow out the power of our adversary against us.

Ephesians 6:10 says that we should "be strong in the Lord and in the power of His might." The Greek word for power in this verse is kratos (krat'-os), meaning dominion, strength, manifested power.[9] Not just the power within us,

---

[7] Strong, James. "973 βιαστής (biastés)," Strong's Greek: 973. βιαστής (biastés) (BibleHub, 2023), https://biblehub.com/greek/strongs/973.htm.
[8] Strong, James. "1411 δύναμις (dunamis)," Strong's Greek: 1411. δύναμις (dunamis) (BibleHub, 2023), https://biblehub.com/greek/strongs/1411.htm.
[9] Strong, James. "2904 κράτος (kratos)," Strong's Greek: 2904. κράτος (kratos) (BibleHub, 2023), https://biblehub.com/greek/strongs/2904.htm.

but the power of our Advocate coming out of us to take dominion over the power of our adversary. It is the demonstration of our declaration of faith in our Advocate by the power of the Holy Spirit. Again, this goes all the way back to the beginning, where God gave the man and woman kratos, dominion over every living thing that moves upon the earth. This is what the Lord Jesus came to the earth for—to restore to us kingdom dominion over all the power of the adversary, over all the power of sinful flesh, over all the power of this world, over all the power of death and the grave. Hallelujah! The question is this: How do we get there, and how is this accomplished in us?

It's one thing to know it, but it's another thing to believe it. How do we come to that level of faith where there is demonstrated, manifested power? As mentioned above, Ephesians 6:10 says to "be strong in the Lord, in the power of His might." How do we get to be strong in the Lord? Isaiah 40:29 says, "He gives power to the weak, and to those who have no might He increases strength." The Lord Jesus says in John 15:5 that He is the vine, and we are the branches, and without Him we can do nothing. When we really come to know how weak we are in ourselves, how helpless we are against our adversary, we will come to know how dependent we are upon our Advocate. This knowledge comes through the trials and tribulations of this life that the Lord Jesus said that we would have.

Our Advocate uses trials to bring us into that place of brokenness where we realize that He is our only hope. He alone is our strength. He alone is our confidence and our help. Without Him, we are nothing but fragile clay pots (2 Cor. 4:7). When we go through trials, when we walk through the valley of the shadow of death, we have the opportunity to really know whether we believe what we say we believe. We can know the Scripture that says that He is a very present help in the time of our trouble (Psalm 46:1), but we have the opportunity to believe it during troubled times.

Isaiah 43:2 says that when we pass through the waters, when we feel like we're in over our head, and about to go under, He will hold us up. We don't really know this and come to believe it until we're in over our head, and all we can do is cry out to our Advocate. When we can't do anything but cry out, then we find out that the rivers of trouble shall not overflow us. We find out that the fire may burn, but not consume us. It will only purify what is impure in us.

In Daniel 3:14–25, Daniel's three friends, Shadrach, Meshach, and Abednego, refuse to bow down to the gold image King Nebuchadnezzar had set up in his own honor. He was enraged at them, threatening to throw them into a fiery furnace heated seven times hotter than usual. He then declared, "and who is the god who will deliver you?" (Verse 15). They confidently declare that it is the God whom they serve—not the God they heard about, read about, or knew about, but the God whom they serve. In essence, they said, "Our God is able to deliver us, but even if He chooses not to deliver us, He is still our God. We are prepared to die serving Him rather than live serving you and the gods of your own creation."

There are times God will prove His love and who He is more than what He is able to do. We are His servants; He is not ours. He is a wonderful, all-knowing Master who always has our best interest at heart. God does not always do what He is able to do. Sometimes He has something else in mind that He intends to do, and that is usually what He intends to do "in us" rather than "for us." Working in us the image and likeness of His Son, who "though He was a Son, yet He learned obedience by the things which He suffered" (Heb. 5:8).

In John 11, the Lord Jesus's friend Lazarus was sick, and his friends asked Jesus to come and heal him. But Jesus did not immediately go as they hoped He would. He stayed where He was two more days, and in that time, Lazarus died. When Jesus finally showed up, Lazarus's sisters both let Him know that if He had been on time, their brother would have lived. God is always on time—His time, not necessarily ours; He's never early and He's never late because time is His servant for His purposes. The Lord Jesus could have showed up earlier and healed Lazarus, but it wasn't the time for that on this occasion. It was the time for something else, and it would exceed the time his sisters were hoping for. It was the time for the Resurrection and the Life to be revealed, a preview of what we have to look forward to for all eternity.

We've all been in a similar situation, where we were hoping for a particular outcome at a particular time, and God doesn't show up. This is when our adversary can try to take advantage of the situation to turn us against our Advocate.

Rather, we need to take advantage of the situation to have greater faith in our Advocate. He is able to make all things work together for the good of them that love Him (Rom. 8:28). The critical question is this: Do I love Him more than what I want from Him?

God created us out of love—for Him to love us and for us to love Him. His love for us is never-ending and unfailing. Can ours for Him be any less, whatever it costs us? In Philippians 3:8, the Apostle Paul said, "I also count all things loss for the excellence of the knowledge of Christ Jesus my Lord, for whom I have suffered the loss of all things, and count them as rubbish, that I may gain Christ." Again, it's one thing to say that when I still have what I have; it's another thing to say it when I don't have it.

Romans 1:17 says that the just shall live by faith, which is a quote from Habakkuk 2:4 in the Old Testament. However, in the New Testament, our faith is in the Lord Jesus, to which the whole Old Testament points.

> *But now the righteousness of God apart from*
> *the law is revealed, being witnessed by the Law*
> *and the Prophets, even the righteousness of God,*
> *through faith in Jesus Christ,*
> *to all and on all who believe.*
>
> (Rom. 3:21–22)

So, the life we live in this world is by the faith of the Son of God which brings us back to Shadrach, Meshach, and Abednego. They maintained their faith in the God they served despite the fact that He did not show up in time to stop their adversary from casting them into a fiery furnace. Just because God does not show up when we expect Him to does not mean that He's not going to show up. As a matter of fact, our Advocate often shows up when we least expect it.

We can see that in the case of the three Hebrew servants. God did not show up to deliver them from the furnace, but He did show up in the furnace. "King Nebuchadnezzar was astonished…'Did we not cast three men bound into the midst of the fire…I see four men loose, walking in the midst of the fire; and they are not hurt, and the form of the fourth is like the Son of God'" (Dan. 3:24–25). Remember, this fire was stoked up seven times hotter so that it even killed the men who cast them into the fire, and yet the four figures walked around as though they were taking a stroll in the park. Our faith in God is never more confirmed than when He meets us in the fiery trials and troubled waters of this life that threaten to consume us. Our adversary is forced to acknowledge that He is God. He is forced to acknowledge that no weapon he formed against us can prosper as long as our faith in our Advocate remains steadfast. The accusatory tongue of our adversary will be silenced again and again (Isa. 54:17).

Faith in God is what most pleases God, and when that is so, Proverbs 16:7 says the Lord, our Advocate, makes even our enemies (adversaries) be at peace with us. In fact, James 4:7 says that when we humbly submit ourselves in faith to God, we can resist our adversary and "he will flee from us."

We now turn to Job as a prime example of the "Frontal Attack." We might say that the frontal attack is characterized by four Ps: our possessions, our person, our position, and our purpose.

> *Now there was a day when the sons of God came to present themselves before the Lord, and Satan also came among them. And the Lord said to Satan, "From where do you come?" So Satan answered the Lord and said, "From going to and fro on the earth, and from walking back and forth on it." Then the Lord said to Satan, "Have you considered My servant Job, that there is none like him on the earth, a blameless and upright man, one who fears God and shuns evil?" So Satan answered the Lord and said, "Does Job fear God for nothing? Have you not made a hedge around him, around his household, and around all that he has on every side? You have blessed the work of his hands, and his possessions have increased in the land. But now, stretch out Your hand and touch all that he has, and he will surely curse You to Your face!" And the Lord said to Satan, "Behold, all that he has is in your power; only do not lay a hand on his person." So Satan went out from the presence of the Lord.*
>
> (Job 1:6–12)

This is a heavenly scene, and the "sons of God" spoken of in verse six are most likely angels, servants of God.

Let us take note of a few things. First of all, God asks Satan where he came from. The adversary responds, "from going to and fro on the earth." Our adversary is a restless prowler, seeking whom he may devour (1 Pet. 5:8). Secondly, he is an observer, particularly of the those who walk upright with a perfect heart toward the Lord. Thirdly, our adversary may not touch our possessions, person, position, or purpose without permission. He must come before the Lord with his case, and that is really the heart of the matter. Remember, Revelation 12:10 refers to our adversary as "the accuser of our brethren [brothers and sisters in Christ], who accused them before our God day and night." He is determined to prove that our motives for serving God are only for our own benefit—only because of what He can do for us, not Who He is to us. In other words, our motives are imperfect and impure. However, our Advocate is more determined to prove just the opposite in allowing him to touch what we have.

So, it should not surprise us that the prime targets of the adversary are those who walk upright before the Lord, have a holy hedge of protection around us, and are blessed with abundance. Neither should it surprise us if our Advocate should allow our adversary to touch it and take it away, as First Peter 4:12 says, "Beloved, do not think it strange concerning the fiery trial which is to try you, as though some strange thing happened to you." When God said to Satan, "have you considered my servant Job?," that can also be translated, "do you have your eye on him, have you set your heart on him?" God knew from the outset what the adversary had up his sleeve, and He was prepared to prove him wrong. We must understand that we are the proving ground.

Psalm 34:19 says, "Many are the afflictions of the righteous, but the Lord delivers him out of them all." We might add, "…after He proves that we are who He says we are." God declared Job perfect and upright in His sight, and He was prepared to prove it. When we accept the righteousness of Christ as our righteousness, God is prepared to prove it to our adversary when he challenges it.

The word for righteous in the Greek is dikaios (dik'-ah-yos). It means upright, virtuous, keeping the commandments of God.[10] One whose way of **thinking, feeling,** and **acting** is wholly conformed to the will of God. These are the ones that the adversary sets his sights on. These are the ones who are, more often than not, going to be hit with the frontal attack.

God declares to Satan that there is none like Job on the earth, a blameless and upright man, one who needs no rectification in heart or life. He didn't do anything wrong. No wonder he was such a target of the adversary and such a treasure of the Advocate. This is where we can stumble if we don't understand why our Advocate would allow his treasures to be subjected to such treatment from the adversary. God uses His treasures to slay His adversary. No one

---

[10] Strong, James. "1342 δίκαιος (dikaios)," Strong's Greek: 1342. δίκαιος (dikaios) (BibleHub, 2023), https://biblehub.com/greek/strongs/1342.htm.

was more treasured than His only begotten Son whom He allowed to be slain to slay the adversary. And after the adversary was slain by the blood of the Lamb, the Lamb of God was raised from the dead. The adversary, however, will be cast into the lake of fire.

When troubles come and we suffer loss, we, like Job, can begin to ask, "What did I do to deserve this? Why is this happening to me?" There are certainly times when we suffer the consequences of our own wrong actions. We suffer because of sin. However, there are times when we suffer because of what we've done right; we suffer for righteousness at the hand of our adversary, and we can wrestle with it trying to figure it out like Job did. We need not bother, as difficult as that may be, if we have searched our hearts and know that we are right before our Advocate.

> *And who is he who will harm you if you become followers of what is good? But even if you should suffer for righteousness' sake, you are blessed. 'And do not be afraid of their threats, nor be troubled.' For it is better, if it is the will of God, to suffer for doing good than for doing evil.*
>
> (1 Pet. 3:13–14, 17)

Our Advocate will always come to our aid and cause us to ultimately triumph over our adversary. This is where our faith in God comes in. This is where our faith goes from the conceptual to the actual.

> *Though now for a little while, if need be, you have been grieved by various trials, that the genuineness of your faith, being much more precious than gold that perishes, though it is tested by fire, may be found to praise, honor and glory at the revelation of Jesus Christ.*
>
> (1 Pet. 1:6–7)

It is through the trials and tribulations that our faith in our Advocate is proven to be genuine and real. Our faith is more than fair-weather faith. Our Advocate is committed to making us all-weather believers, because He knows that the weather in this world is not always fair. What could be more unfair than the pure, holy, sinless Son of God being crucified when He had done no wrong? Crucifixion was a penalty reserved for only the worst of criminals.

Even Pilate was determined to release Him, because he said, "I find no fault in Him at all" (John 18:38). However, there was an adversary who was more determined to incite the crowd to crucify Him. But this only proved that He was who His Father said He was, "My beloved Son, in whom I am well pleased" (Matt. 3:17). Even the Roman centurion who watched Him take His final breath exclaimed, "Surely, this was the Son of God." Whatever the weather, we will be proven to be believers in the Lord Jesus Christ if we hold fast to our faith in Him.

In fact, the apostle Peter goes on to say in First Peter 5:10, "May the God of all grace, who called us to His eternal glory by Christ Jesus, after you have suffered a while, perfect, establish, strengthen, and settle you." I'm so glad that our God has an after. He doesn't leave us in the suffering. He didn't leave His beloved Son in the tomb. He brought Him forth with resurrection power, and that same power brings us forth perfected, established, strengthened, and settled.

We now return to the adversary's response to God's declaration of His servant Job's righteousness in Job 1:9–11. This is a crucial test for every believer in the Lord Jesus Christ. What is my motive for following Him? Our adversary will always try to accuse us of having selfish motives as he did in Job's case, suggesting that his good behavior was only for what he could get from God, not for God, Himself. "Let me take it all away from him, and he'll curse You to Your face." That's a bold and brazen accusation, that Job would curse God to His face. Who would dare to do that except someone who had the same spirit as the adversary? In verse twelve God says OK. He grants the adversary permission to take it all away from him but restricts him from laying a hand upon Job. It is crucial for us to understand that if our Advocate allows our adversary to touch what and who belongs to us, it is to accomplish His purposes, to prove that we are His, come what may, that we love Him for who He is with all of our heart, mind, soul, and strength.

Our Advocate knows that our faith must be more than our words; it must be more than our religion; it must be our entire life. The Lord Jesus said of the religious leaders and their followers of His day in Matthew 15:8 (quoting from Isaiah 29:13), "These people…honor Me with their lips [words], but their heart is far from Me." And not only that, but we are being conformed to the image and likeness of the Lord whom we proclaim—who, "though He was a Son, yet He learned obedience by the things which He suffered" (Heb. 5:8). We learn and we are conformed in the same way.

Philippians 2:5 says, "Let this mind be in you which was also in Christ Jesus." Verse eight goes on to say, "He humbled Himself and became obedient to the point of death, even the death of the cross." But it didn't end there. It was only the means to a greater end. For verse nine tells us, "Therefore God also has highly exalted Him and given Him the name which is above every name." If we are ever going to know the power of the great Name of the Lord Jesus, we will have to be willing to humble ourselves under His mighty Hand. We will have to be obedient even to the point of death to this world with all its enticements. We will have to die to our will, desires, and plans until there is nothing left of us, but only Him. This may sound like a lofty ideal, but the Holy Spirit in us can make it real, if we are willing. As far as the apostle Paul was concerned, this was the goal of our salvation, as he states in Philippians 3:13–14, "One thing I do, forgetting those things which are behind and reaching forward to those things which are ahead, I press toward the goal for the prize of the upward call of God in Christ Jesus." Rather than "press," we can "be pressed" if we are willing.

We have four children, three boys and a girl. On September 29, 1998, the date of our youngest son's twenty-first birthday, our oldest son, Jeffrey, our firstborn, who was a second-year law student at Boston University, went out for a ride on his bicycle after classes—something he often did to unwind. This time, something went terribly wrong. For some reason, he flipped over the handlebars and ended up with blunt-force trauma to his head. We received a call from the emergency room of Beth Israel Deaconess hospital around eight thirty that evening, telling us of the accident and requesting permission to do emergency surgery to relieve the bleeding and swelling of his brain—the God-given brain that enabled him to be in the top 10 percent of his class, the brain that meditated on the Word of God. The neurosurgeon told us he should be "fine" once the surgery was done. However, when we got to Boston around three thirty the next morning, he was not "fine." They took him back into surgery. When they came out of surgery around eight o'clock in the morning, they informed us that there was no more they could do, and he would probably not survive the day.

The adversary said, "Let me take their firstborn son from them, and they will curse you to your face." We had people all over the country praying that God would heal him and raise him up. We surrounded his bedside throughout that Wednesday, September 30th. I took a nap about ten o'clock that night. I woke up around one o'clock the following morning, Thursday, October 1. I went back into his room, and once again, looked at all the tubes attached to him, including a tube breathing for him, and all of a sudden it hit me. He was engaged in a valiant fight to stay alive not for his own sake, but for ours. I realized that we had to release him to the One who gave him and to whom he truly belonged. I walked over to his bed, where he lay unconscious and spoke into his ear, "Son, if you have seen the face of Jesus, you do what the Father tells you." And that was it. The grace of the Advocate enabled me to humble myself under his mighty hand and acknowledge that Jeffrey was His son more than he was ours. My wife came into the room, and I told her what I had done. She said, "The Lord showed me that while you were sleeping, and I did the same thing." That settled it.

While we sat at his bedside, all of a sudden, my wife grabbed my arm and exclaimed, "Did you see that? I just saw Jesus and Jeffrey, and they both were dressed in white robes, and Jeffrey was perfect like I've never seen him before. He had all his hair back (which had been shaved off for the surgeries). Jesus had his arms open and said to Jeffrey, 'Welcome. Well done, good and faithful servant. Enter into the joy of your Lord.'"

I said to her, "You mean you pictured that or imagined it in your mind?" She went on to explain that it was like a curtain had been pulled back, and she saw the whole thing with her natural eyes. She also told me that at that moment she felt an indescribable peace that she had never experienced before. "I know that it will be the peace we will have forever with the Lord in heaven." This was the glory and the divine intervention of the Advocate. Right after that, the doctor came in and examined him and proclaimed there was no longer any brain activity. Jeffrey was gone.

A frontal attack from our adversary, whom I sincerely believe was betting on the fact that if he were permitted to take our firstborn from us, we would curse God to His face. In Old Testament times, the firstborn son held a privileged position. He received the double portion as the first fruits of the union between husband and wife. However, the first fruits can also be an offering to God to honor him as the Lord of the harvest, the Lord as our source and giver of all life. In Exodus 13:2, God spoke to Moses saying, "Consecrate [set apart] to Me all the firstborn, whatever opens the womb among the children of Israel, both of man and beast; it is Mine."

When we bring our children to the church shortly after their birth, to dedicate them to the Lord, we are publicly declaring that they belong to God, they are rightfully His. This is in keeping with the example of Joseph and Mary bringing the child Jesus to the temple eight days after his birth to dedicate Him to the Lord.

There is a special bond we have with our firstborn child. We go through the first of everything with them. They lead the way. So it was with our firstborn. He led the way for his siblings. He loved them intensely, and they looked up to him with great admiration.

Like Job, this was not our first frontal attack.

Nearly twenty-three years earlier, on December 3, 1975, six days after the birth of our second son, Joshua, we were involved in a violent car crash on our way to his first postnatal doctor visit. My wife had been holding him in the front passenger seat. Upon impact, he dislodged from her arms, smashed his head against the dashboard, and rolled under the front seat. My wife and I were both knocked unconscious. Authorities were about to tow the car away when they heard our baby whimpering under the seat. He barely survived. Joshua suffered acquired hydrocephalus with left side hemiplegia, requiring nearly twenty major operations throughout his infancy and growing up years. Going to school and socializing were extremely challenging for him. He was not a happy camper, but he (and we) pressed on. His older brother, Jeffrey, was a key to pressing on. He became Joshua's best and only friend. When we had to tell Jeffrey's siblings, on the morning of October 1, 1998, that he was gone, we will never forget the look of incredible horror on our second son's face. Our last born, our daughter, who was fifteen at the time, threw herself across his lifeless body and pleaded with him to wake up! Our third born son was numb with grief. The pain of that moment was simply staggering. To this day, even at this writing, it still brings me to tears.

> *"And the dragon [our adversary] was enraged with the woman, and he went to make war with the rest of her offspring, who keep the commandments of God and have the testimony of Jesus Christ."*
>
> (Rev. 12:17)

Job kept the Commandments of God and diligently watched over his house. It was his house, his offspring, his possessions that the adversary attacked, betting that he would curse God to his face. He did not. And so, the first P of the frontal attack, his possessions.

In Job 1:20–22, Job humbled himself, fell to the ground and worshipped. In part, he said, "Naked I came from my mother's womb, and naked shall I return there. The Lord gave, and the Lord has taken away." Job did not blame God for what happened or claim that He did him wrong. He did not curse Him to His face, as his adversary said he would. And yet, I'm not sure whether Job was aware that this was a heavenly battle between his Advocate and his adversary—a battle over whose word would prevail concerning Job. The same is true for us who belong to God. No matter what we suffer, our adversary's word will never prevail over the Word of our Advocate.

Again, believers in Christ must understand that there will be times when we suffer for his name's sake. We must shore up our allegiance to Him, lest we fall prey to the adversary's plot to turn us against our Advocate and curse Him to His face. Our Advocate is committed to confirming our allegiance to him, and proving to us and our adversary that greater is He that is in us than he who is against us.

In Acts 5:40, the apostles were beaten for preaching and healing a lame man in the name of Jesus. However, they were not beaten, nor were they defeated or silenced, because they were glad to be counted worthy to suffer shame for His name.

In Revelation 12:11, it says that we overcome our adversary by the "blood of the Lamb [Jesus] and by the word of [our] testimony." When the Holy Spirit works in us to that degree, it is over for our adversary. However, he won't stop trying, because he's blinded by his hatred for God and His followers.

As we return to Job, he is clinging to his faith in God in the face of unimaginable loss. However, this is only phase one, the first P of the frontal attack. In Job chapter two, Satan again presents himself before the Lord, and He repeats his declaration concerning his servant Job, that there is no one like him on the face of the earth, blameless and upright. In verse three, the Lord states, "And still he holds fast to his integrity, although you [the adversary] incited Me against him, to destroy him without cause."

There is a key here. The adversary was determined to prove that Job did not really love God for God's sake, but for his own sake and benefit. This was not true of Job. God declared it by pronouncing that Job's trouble was without cause.

In other words, he was without fault, and didn't do anything to deserve it. However, I believe that God allowed the frontal attack to elevate Job to another level.

God said of Job, "Still he holds fast to his integrity." But when you read further into the book of Job, his integrity is not going to be enough, and I believe this is what God was after in relation to Job. God took him beyond his integrity and into the unfathomable, incomprehensible realm of

His creation. Job spends chapter upon chapter attempting to bring God down to his level of understanding, which was kind of a quid pro quo understanding—if I do this, God is obligated to do that.

We will never bring God down to our level of understanding. It is too finite and limited compared to the infinite wisdom of God. He is far beyond our comprehension, just as eternity is. God commends Job for holding fast to his integrity, and yet, at the end of the book, God reproves him for darkening His counsel with words without knowledge (Job 38:2). Again, he was trying to bring God down to his level of understanding. Job thought, This should not be happening to me. I am a man of integrity. I haven't done anything to deserve this. It would be different if I had sinned or done wrong, but I haven't. Have you ever been there? Have you felt that way? You've taken the Lord Jesus into your heart. You have committed your life to him, and made every effort to live for him, then whammo! Trouble comes, tragedy comes, difficulties come, and you don't know why. Our adversary's frontal attack on the righteous is meant to bring us down to the point of cursing God and giving up our faith in him. And yet, from our Advocate's perspective, that is what it is all about. The trials bring us to the end of any faith in our own abilities, integrity, or willfulness and force us to rely on God's integrity, character, wisdom, knowledge, and power.

In the gospel of John, chapter nine, there is a man who was blind from birth, and his disciples ask Jesus whose sin resulted in his blindness, this man's or his parents'. Jesus responded that neither this man nor his parents had sinned, but the blindness was allowed so that the works of God should be revealed in him. Our Advocate has a work to accomplish in us that is far greater than what our adversary seeks to work against us. It is God's desire to reveal to the world around us that what He has done in us only He could do, and all for His glory. The wonder of it is that He turns the work of our adversary, which is meant for evil, into a work of God, which is meant for our good!

As we continue the story of Job, we find that he has not cursed God as the adversary said he would. The adversary comes again before the throne of God to take the frontal attack to another level, an even more personal level. Previously, the Lord had permitted the adversary to touch Job's possessions and children but not Job himself. However, now the adversary wants permission to lay his hand upon Job. "All that a man has he will give for his life," suggests the adversary (Job 2:4). He says, in essence, "Let me at him, and he will surely curse you to your face." God grants Satan permission, but again, restricts him from taking Job's life. So, the adversary attacks the second P, Job's person, tormenting his body with pain.

We have an adversary who, from time to time, can have at us, but he cannot have us. We belong to our Advocate, and no one can pluck us out of his hand. Our adversary does not have free reign to do whatever he pleases against us. He can only do what our Advocate permits him to do. It must pass before Him before it touches us. As painful as the frontal attack may be, we must have the hope that if our Advocate gave his approval, it is for His sovereign purposes. We must come to understand that He is only using our adversary to bring it about.

Jacob, the son of Isaac, who was the promised son of Abraham, had a son named Joseph. Jacob loved Joseph more than all his other children because he was the "Son of his old age" (Gen. 37:3). Jacob made Joseph a coat of many colors such as might be worn by royalty. This could very well have been a prophetic gesture by his father, foretelling the exalted position he would be given in Pharaoh's kingdom thirteen years later. His brothers were jealous of the favoritism their father showed Joseph, and "they hated him and could not speak peaceably to him" (Gen. 37:4). This is the satanic principle, jealousy-inspired hatred toward anyone that has what they do not have. Job enjoyed the favor of God upon his life, and it incited his adversary against him to steal it from him with a frontal attack as he stole it from Adam and Eve with the rear attack.

To make matters even worse for Joseph, he had a couple of dreams depicting him in a position of authoritative reign over his brothers. He told his brothers about the dreams, which further infuriated them. Our adversary despises authority. He is the original rebel and hates anyone in authority over him. He insists on being his own lord. He inspired that same hatred in the religious leaders of Jesus's day as the authority of the Son of God was a threat to their authority, and they could not tolerate that. They conspired to kill him and eventually incited the people to cry, "Crucify him. Crucify him."

Joseph's brothers had the same intentions when they were out in the fields and saw Joseph approaching them in the distance. They conspired to kill him out of jealousy and hatred. The third P, his position of favor with his father, was under attack. We can rest assured that the favor that we enjoy with our heavenly Father because of our devotion to His favorite Son, will come under attack by our adversary. However, we can also rest assured that our Advocate will only use it to strengthen our devotion to His favorite Son and increase His favor upon our life. Romans 8:37 says, "Yet in all these things we are more than conquerors through Him who loved us."

Jacob's first-born son, Reuben, intervened and persuaded his brothers to throw him into a pit in the wilderness with the intent that he would return him afterwards to his father. Have you ever felt like you've been in a "pit in the wilderness"? You didn't know what was happening or how you were ever going to get out. Perhaps you've been in a situation over which you had no control. Joseph must've felt that way. What did I do to deserve this? His brothers decided to sell him as a slave to Midian traders. These traders took him to Egypt, which was exactly where God wanted him to be, even if Joseph didn't want to be there, because this was where the dreams were going to be fulfilled.

However, they would not be fulfilled until the adversary inflicted one more frontal attack upon him. This time, he was falsely accused of sexual assault toward his master's wife and thrown into prison. The fourth P, the attack against his purpose—to be second-in-command in all Egypt to fulfill the calling and purpose of God upon his life. Once again, though, this was exactly according to God's plan, regardless of the plan of the enemy. While he was in prison, Joseph interpreted the dreams of Pharaoh's baker and butler. This encounter would eventually usher him into the presence of Pharaoh. I am sure Joseph never "dreamed" this would be the way God brought about His purposes.

After Joseph interpreted the butler's and baker's dreams, they were released from the prison they shared with Joseph. Upon their release, Joseph asked them to remember him to Pharaoh when their dreams came to pass as he had interpreted. Just as Joseph had said, the baker was put to death and the butler was restored to his position in Pharaoh's kingdom. But the butler forgot about Joseph. Two years later, Pharaoh had vivid dreams that greatly disturbed him, and no one was able to interpret them. It was then that the butler remembered Joseph and his ability to accurately interpret dreams. It would've been easy for Joseph to begin to lose heart, to begin to lose his faith in God, and question whether his dreams would ever come to pass, but he remained faithful until the day he was ushered into Pharaoh's presence.

He interpreted Pharaoh's dreams and instructed him on how he should respond to what was coming. As a result, Joseph was made second-in-command over all of Egypt and put in charge of the disbursement of food supplies during the seven years of famine in Egypt. They were prepared for the seven years of famine because God had given Joseph a plan to carry out during the preceding seven years of abundance. The grand finale was that, through his position in Egypt, he ended up saving the brothers who had conspired to kill him. Genesis 45:7–8 tells of Joseph speaking to his brothers, saying,

> *"God sent me before you to preserve a posterity for you in the earth, and to save your lives by a great deliverance. So now it was not you who sent me here, but God; and He has made me a father to Pharaoh, and lord of all his house, and a ruler throughout all the land of Egypt."*

Joseph goes on to say to his brothers in Genesis 50:20, "You meant evil against me; but God meant it for good." Isn't it amazing that no matter what evil our adversary is permitted to wage against us, our Advocate will turn it for good? Our Advocate always has the last word and makes the final judgment in favor of the saints of the Lord Jesus Christ!

What pit or prison is confining or limiting you right now? What hard place has you stuck? Don't fight or curse it, but be willing to endure it with the knowledge of the glory that's coming, just as the Lord Jesus endured the cross, despising the shame, because he saw the joy that was coming. Just as the apostle Paul most gladly boasted in his hard places that the power and authority of Christ may rest upon him, the high place coming out of the hard place. We need to keep this in mind when the enemy plants doubt in our minds about the dreams that God gave us. I believe that everything Joseph experienced at the hand of his adversary was a time of preparation at the hand of his Advocate—preparation for the position he would occupy and preparation for those that would be saved. Our willingness to endure the preparation for the purpose can mean salvation for others. Even though Joseph was sold as a slave in Potiphar's house, he rose to the top and prospered by becoming his master's right-hand man. Joseph didn't wallow in misery after being unfairly treated and thrown into prison; he served his master and found favor with him. So much so, that he was put in charge of all the rest of the prisoners. God used the hard place of the prison to prepare Joseph for the high place of the palace. In fact, I believe it was the pit and the prison that not only prepared Joseph for the palace but kept him in the palace. The knowledge that our Advocate is preparing us for a higher place can comfort us and keep us from self-pity.

Genesis 39:21 states that the Lord was with Joseph in the prison. More than 400 years later, Moses spoke the words of the Lord to the Israelites, saying, "He will not leave you nor forsake you" (Deut. 31:6) He would always be with them wherever they went, whatever they were facing, and whatever state they were in. They could count on Him, and so can we. The promise is for all who put their faith and trust in Him. That promise was fulfilled on the day of Pentecost when the Holy Spirit was sent to those who expectantly waited for Him. The power of His presence and the person of the Holy Spirit filled the gathering of believers that day. We can rest assured that the Lord Jesus is with us in the hard places. He knows more about hard places than anyone, and yet, He now sits in the high place at the right hand of God, ruling and reigning until all His enemies are made his footstool!

Because God was with Joseph, whatever he did prospered. If God is with us and for us, who can be against us (Rom. 8:31)? The adversity that Joseph suffered was preparation for the fulfillment of the dreams God had given him. He was proven faithful despite the rigors of the pit and the prison, and he learned to prosper in the hard places. True prosperity is developed in the hard places. When we learn to prosper in difficulties, the blessing and favor of our Advocate will be upon us to bring us into the higher places of authority in His kingdom. I believe the measure of authority we have as believers in Christ Jesus is directly related to our willingness to do His will and come under His authority. God brought Joseph out of the pit, and out of the prison, and into the higher place. If we want to go higher, into the place God has called us to, we will have to go harder to prove our fitness and faithfulness for the higher place. The beauty is that God makes us forget the hard place when He brings us into the high place. Our sorrow will be turned into joy, and our weakness into strength, and our poverty into the riches of His grace.

And to Joseph were born two sons....Joseph called the name of the firstborn Manasseh [which means "making forgetful"]: "For God has made me forget all my toil and all my father's house." And the name of the second he called Ephraim [which means "fruitfulness"]: "For God has caused me to be fruitful in the land of my affliction."

(Gen. 41:50–52)

We will explore this further in the next chapter as we look into the life of the apostle Paul, who wrote more Holy Spirit-inspired letters to the church than any other apostle.

Chapter Three

The Glory and the Story

*You see the glory,
but you don't know the story.*

unknown

Wherever you see His glory, you can rest assured there's a story behind it. The Lord Jesus said to His disciples in Luke 24:25–26, "O foolish ones, and slow of heart to believe… Ought not the Christ to have suffered these things and to enter into His glory?" The apostle Paul said, in Romans 8:18, "For I consider that the sufferings of this present time are not worthy to be compared with the glory which shall be revealed in us."

Crowns follow crosses, and glory follows sufferings. I am not sure whether you could have a crown without a cross or know His glory without having had fellowship with His sufferings. The sufferings will come, with permission, at the hand of our adversary, but will give way to the glory of our Advocate. The hope we have enables us to believe and not lose heart. We must know that at some point suffering will come. The Lord Jesus said, "If they persecuted Me, they also will persecute you" (John 15:20). Of course, we know that our adversary inspired the persecutors. First Peter 2:21 says, "For to this [unjust suffering] you were called, because Christ also suffered for us, leaving us an example, that you should follow His steps."

Such was the case for me. In January 1995, I served as President/CEO of a local branch of a national Christian social service agency. Several employees were disgruntled over decisions I had made and conspired together to go to the governing board and bring charges against me. The governing board did not know what to do and brought in the regional vice president, whom I believe had viewed me as a little too "Christian" for the agency and now had the opportunity to replace me. I advised the board of my reasons for the decisions in question. Nevertheless, I was fired. Before they made their decision, the Lord spoke very clearly to me that the vice president was "selling me down the river." I didn't know what I was going to do, but the Lord assured me that this was not their doing, but His. They only did what God had determined beforehand, because He was changing the course of my life. It would not have happened had He not determined it. God determines our way in our history if we are willing to be pliable in His hands, like the clay with the potter.

God, our Advocate, may allow us to pursue our own ambitions for a season, but when it's time to get on with

His ambitions and His plan, He may use our adversary's work against us to accomplish His will. This is the higher way for followers of Christ. Suffering for doing wrong is the lower, corrective way. Hopefully, we learned from it and we don't repeat it. But the higher way is the glory way. It brings the manifestation and demonstration of His glory in and through us.

> *Then Saul, still breathing threats and murder against the disciples of the Lord, went to the high priest and asked letters from him to the synagogues of Damascus, so that if he found any who were of the Way, whether men or women, he might bring them bound to Jerusalem.*
> *As he journeyed, he came near Damascus, and suddenly a light shown around him from heaven. Then he fell to the ground, and heard a voice saying to him, "Saul, Saul, why are you persecuting Me?" And he said, "Who are you, Lord?" Then the Lord said, "I am Jesus, whom you are persecuting. It is hard for you to kick against the goads." So he, trembling and astonished, said, "Lord, what do you want me to do?" Then the Lord said to him, "arise and go into the city, and you will be told what you must do."*
> *And the men who journeyed with him stood speechless, hearing a voice but seeing no one. Then Saul arose from the ground, and when his*

> *eyes were opened, he saw no one. But they led him by the hand and brought him into Damascus. And he was three days without sight, and neither ate nor drank.*
>
> *Now there was a certain disciple at Damascus named Ananias; and to him the Lord said in a vision, "Ananias." And he said, "Here I am, Lord." So the Lord said to him, "Arise and go to the street called Straight, and inquire at the house of Judas for one called Saul of Tarsus, for behold, he is praying. And in a vision he has seen a man named Ananias coming in and putting his hand on him, so that he might receive his sight."*
>
> *Then Ananias answered, "Lord, I have heard from many about this man, how much harm he has done to your saints in Jerusalem. And here he has authority from the chief priests to bind all who call on your name."*
>
> *But the Lord said to him, "Go, for he is a chosen vessel of Mine to bear My name before Gentiles, kings, and the children of Israel. For I will show him how many things he must suffer for My name's sake."*
>
> (Acts 9:1–16)

Saul, before he was transformed into the apostle Paul, was a tool of the adversary to persecute the church, which belonged to the Advocate. Saul was a servant of the adversary.

The irony of it was that Saul believed he was serving God by eliminating those he believed to be blasphemers of his God. We see a parallel to the head of the church, Christ, who was crucified for the same reason.

Second Corinthians 4:4 says that the God of this age, the adversary, blinds the minds of unbelievers, lest the light of the gospel should shine upon them. We can all say that our minds were blinded and we served the adversary until the light of the gospel shone in our hearts. God, our Advocate, was so merciful to enlighten us, lest we still be held captive by our adversary. It's amazing to consider that he was our Advocate before we ever knew Him.

Jesus was the "Lamb slain from the foundation of the world" (Rev. 13:8). Before the world was formed, before we were formed. The Lord Jesus says in Revelation 1:8, "I am the Alpha and the Omega, the Beginning and the End." Our Advocate started it all, and He will end it all. He has already guaranteed the ending with the cross. He declared, "It is finished." The Lord Jesus finished it all on the cross. There was nothing He left unfinished—no sin, no death, no grave, no fear, no failure, no trouble, no tragedy. All of it was finished and covered by the cross of the Lord Jesus. We don't ever have to worry about anything. He has it all covered. Sooner or later, it is all covered by the cross.

We can have all confidence in our Advocate's knowledge of the beginning and the end. Whatever our adversary throws at us, we know that our Advocate has permitted it in accordance with His advanced knowledge. He works everything together for our good, as Romans 8:28 says, according to his purpose, overriding and overruling the purpose of our adversary. The Greek word for purpose in this verse is prothesis (proth'-es-is) which means a setting forth, a deliberate, advanced plan.[11] Our Advocate knew the plans of every man, woman, and devil before they were ever planned. He planned accordingly to make them conform to His purposes and His will. He will bring everything into line with His will because He is the end; He has the last word. We can have this confidence in our Advocate.

Acts 4:27–28 says, "For truly against Your holy Servant Jesus, whom You anointed, both Herod and Pontius pilot, with the Gentiles and the people of Israel, were gathered together to do whatever Your hand and Your purpose determined before to be done." They only did whatever the hand and the purpose of God had already determined beforehand should be done to ultimately bring about his will and his purpose—the salvation of the world.
And this came to pass in Paul's life:

> *"Are they ministers of Christ? —I speak as a fool—I am more: in labors more abundant, in stripes above measure, in prisons more frequently, in deaths often. From the Jews five times I received forty stripes minus one. Three times I was*

---

[11] Strong, James. "4286 πρόθεσις (prothesis)," Strong's Greek: 4286. πρόθεσις (prothesis) (BibleHub, 2023), https://biblehub.com/greek/strongs/4286.htm.

beaten with rods; once I was stoned; three times I was shipwrecked; a night and a day I have been in the deep; in journeys often, in perils of waters, in perils of robbers, in perils of my own countrymen, in perils of the Gentiles, in perils in the city, in perils in the wilderness, in perils in the sea, in perils among false brethren; in weariness and toil, in sleeplessness often, in hunger and thirst, in fastings often, in cold and nakedness."

(2 Cor. 11:23–27)

The apostle Paul received stripes similar to the Lord Jesus, and "by His stripes we are healed." Stripes refers to being beaten with a cord of leather strands with bits of jagged bone and metal that cut into the back of the one being beaten. Not only that, but Acts 14:19–20 suggests that Paul was very possibly stoned to death, but "rose up and went into the city." The apostle Paul often went without sleep and food. On several occasions, he was put in prison. This is where he wrote, under the inspiration of the Holy Spirit, many letters which we read in the Bible today. The adversary may have incited the rulers to imprison him, but God intended it as a sacred place to bring forth the very words of life from our Advocate.

As Paul says in Second Timothy 2:9, even though he suffered as an evildoer and was put in chains, the Word of God could not be chained by the adversary. This is important for us to know when we find ourselves in a binding situation that hems us in. His Word will prevail and bring release.

Paul speaks of us as ministers of God in Second Corinthians 6:8–10, where it says, "By honor and dishonor, by evil report and good report; as deceivers, and yet true; as unknown, and yet well known; as dying, and behold we live; as chastened, and yet not killed; as sorrowful, yet always rejoicing; as poor, yet making many rich; as having nothing, and yet possessing all things." The apostle Paul was eventually beheaded for the sake of Christ while in prison, and yet two-thirds of the New Testament was written by him.

We return to Saul on the road to Damascus. As he journeyed, and came near Damascus, a light from heaven shown around him, and he fell to the ground. He was slain by the light of the Word, the Lord Jesus, who spoke to Saul asking why he was persecuting Him. Saul was being called to account for his actions against the One whom he thought he was defending, and all he could say was, "Who are you, Lord?" Saul didn't have to guess whether it was the Lord, he just had to know His name, and His name is Jesus. Saul was trembling and astonished just as the devil and his angels trembled, but unlike them, Saul asks, "Lord, what do you want me to do?" He was undone by the Lord Jesus.

Saul immediately acknowledges Jesus as Lord, and repents, turning from his murderous way to go where the Lord Jesus would have him go. Jesus tells him to continue on his way. He is now going to be a chosen instrument of promotion rather than persecution of the Lord Jesus. He would now become an instrument of the Advocate, and no longer an instrument of the adversary. As an instrument of the Advocate, he would build up the church and help it advance across the earth, glorifying the Head of the church. There would be great glory in and through the church, but there would also be a story behind the glory.

When Saul got up from the ground, he was blind and had to be led by the hand. He was a converted Saul who would become Paul, an apostle of the Lord Jesus Christ.

Saul arrived in Damascus blind and remained that way for three days until the Lord spoke to Ananias in a vision. He told Ananias to go to Saul and lay his hands upon him and pray for him to receive his sight. The light of Jesus's glory was so bright that it blinded Saul to the way he was going—his way was a destructive way, but he didn't know this. There are times in our lives when we are going the wrong way, and we don't know it, and God will show up with great glory that brings us to our knees and stops us dead in our tracks. It leaves us saying, "Lord, what would you have me to do?" He has our attention, and we are willing to wait on Him to open our eyes.

Such was the case with Saul, and also Ananias, who feared Saul in the beginning and did not want to do what the Lord asked him to do. Ananias feared for his own life, "but the Lord said to him, 'Go, for he is a chosen vessel of Mine to bear My name before Gentiles, kings, and the children of Israel'" (Acts 9:15). The very name Saul had persecuted, he would now be promoting.

Paul would face strong opposition from the adversary. Consequently, a price to pay. "For I will show him how many things he must suffer for My name's sake" (Acts 9:16). The Lord Jesus was preparing him ahead of time that there was going to be strong opposition to his declaration of Jesus as Lord and that would cause him to suffer.

Later, in Romans 8:18, Saul, now renamed Paul (meaning "humble"), would boldly declare that the "sufferings of this present time are not worthy to be compared with the glory which shall be revealed in us." Later in Acts, we see that the Holy Spirit continues to make Paul aware of the sufferings that await him.

> *"And see, now I go bound in the spirit to Jerusalem, not knowing the things that will happen to me there, except that the Holy Spirit testifies in every city, saying that chains and tribulations await me. But none of these things move me; nor do I count my life dear to myself, so that I may finish my race with joy, and the ministry which I received from the Lord Jesus, to testify to the gospel of the grace of God."*
> (Acts 20:22-24)

Through the ministry to which he's been called, and by the grace of God, he's going to finish his race and finish it with joy—the joy that comes from knowing that his life is a pleasure to his God and King. The Bible says that we are not ignorant of our adversary's strategies. I believe one of his primary strategies is to keep us from the ministry God has called us to. Having the Holy Spirit enlighten us with the knowledge of our ministry enables us to stand strong when our adversary subjects us to troubles, trials, and hardship. The attacks of the adversary should only strengthen our resolve not to be moved, because we know we're on the right track with our Advocate. Our adversary does not have to bother with those who are on the wrong track; he is primarily interested with those who are on the right track and present the greatest threat to his kingdom.

Second Timothy 3:12 says, "all who desire to live godly in Christ Jesus will suffer persecution." Paul is reminding his spiritual son Timothy that all who choose to live a godly life in Christ Jesus will suffer persecution, either directly or indirectly. So, we must not be surprised, as though some strange thing is happening to us. It is not strange if we understand that we have an Advocate and an adversary. An Advocate who apprehended us as His chosen, choice vessel, as the apostle Peter says in First Peter 2:9. We are a chosen generation to bear the name of our Advocate, and we have an adversary who knows who we are.

The word chosen can mean the best of its kind, picked out from among many. Chosen people have been proven and are willing to be qualified. The Lord Jesus said in Matthew 22:14 that many are called, but few are chosen or willing to be qualified or proven. They are the ones the adversary fears the most and seeks to take out, but our Advocate only uses his efforts to raise them up to a level of authority so that they can take the adversary out. That level of authority does not come without a price. We must have a willingness to lose our lives in order to gain the full authority of His life. We must have a willingness to not love our lives even unto death. As mentioned earlier, Acts 19:14–16 tells the story of the seven sons of a Jewish priest named Sceva, who tried to exorcise an evil spirit by using the name of Jesus. The evil spirit responded by saying, "Jesus I know, and Paul I know; but who are you?" Then the man in whom the evil spirit dwelt leapt upon them all and gave them such a beating that it left them naked and bleeding. Our adversary knows the difference between the chosen ones who carry His authority, and the ones who know Him in name only.

To be a chosen one of the Lord Jesus comes with a price, but it ultimately comes with a prize, the upward call of God in Christ Jesus. The upward call is to be seated with Christ in heavenly places, ruling and reigning with Him until all His enemies, and ours, are made footstools. It is a place of high authority over our adversary. The evil spirit said that he knew Paul—what he knew was that the apostle Paul had proven authority over him. Paul had proven his authority by the things he suffered at the adversary's hand and the fact that he had come out more than a conqueror through Him who loved him.

This is all our Advocate's doing. We can never take any credit for it. In the apostle Paul's case, this was made very clear to him in Second Corinthians 12:7-10

And lest I should be exalted above measure by the abundance of the revelations, a thorn in the flesh was given to me, a messenger of Satan to buffet me, lest I be exalted above measure. Concerning this thing I pleaded with the Lord three times that it might depart from me. And He said to me, "My grace is sufficient for you, for My strength is made perfect in weakness." Therefore most gladly I will rather boast in my infirmities, that the power of Christ may rest upon me. Therefore, I take pleasure in infirmities, in reproaches, in needs, in persecutions, in distresses, for Christ's sake. For when I am weak, then I am strong.

This thorn in the flesh didn't come from God, but from the adversary given permission by God. Its purpose was to keep Paul from being puffed up with pride and being exalted above measure, which would cause his downfall.

First Peter 4:1–2 says that since Christ suffered for us in the flesh, we should arm ourselves with the same mind. In other words, we are going to suffer in the flesh, as Christ did, but the Scripture goes on to say that we should no longer live the rest of our lives for the lusts of men, but for the will of God.

I am convinced that the pride of success is more dangerous than the humility of failure, trouble, distress, or tribulation. Pride leads to destruction and to the loss of favor with God; humility is constructive and leads to favor with

God. He gives grace, or favor, to the humble, but resists the proud. If we fall prey to the adversary and become puffed up with pride, as Adam and Eve did, our Advocate will become our adversary out of necessity to correct and bring us back into His favor.

Paul pleads with the Lord three times to take the pain of the thorn away. Have you ever been there? You are suffering physically, mentally, emotionally, relationally, or financially, and you just want Him to take it away. What is His response to Paul? "And He said to me." Oh, it's life when God speaks to us! It enlightens us and carries us through the adversity, pain, trouble, distress, and tribulation. When God does not deliver us from it, He is faithful to deliver us in it. He says to his servant Paul, "My grace is sufficient for you, for My strength is made perfect in weakness" (2 Cor. 12:9).

God reveals a profound principle to Paul here. If we are ever going to be useful to God and used by God, we are going to have to learn this principle not so much by the letter, but more by the life in the crucible of physical distress, trouble, and tribulation. If a preacher is ever going to preach with fire, he or she needs to be willing to go through the fire.

Let us return to the story of Shadrach, Meshach, and Abednego. These were three Hebrews living in the land of Babylon and serving, along with Daniel, under the rule of King Nebuchadnezzar. King Nebuchadnezzar had a gold statue erected and gave orders that when the music started, everyone was to fall down and worship the image. A fiery furnace waited for anyone who did not obey. Shadrach,

Meshach, and Abednego were among the conscientious objectors. They made it very clear that they were not going to serve the king's gods or bow down to his gold statue. They were living in obedience to the ten commandments given to Moses, including the very first one, "You shall have no other gods before Me. You shall not make for yourself a carved image…you shall not bow down to them nor serve them" (Ex. 20:3–5).

These three Hebrews let the king know that the God whom they served was able to deliver them from the furnace of his fury, but even if He chose not to, they were still not going to bow down to his gods or his statue. Now at this present time, they enjoyed the favor of occupying high positions in the king's administration. It would have been very tempting for them to go through the motions and satisfy the king's command in order to retain their high positions. However, they were not servants of their positions, they were servants of their God, who is much higher than their positions. This greatly infuriated the king, and his attitude toward them changed. (Have you ever experienced an attitude change from someone with whom you once enjoyed favor?) Shadrach, Meshach, and Abednego were bound, fully dressed, and thrown into the fiery furnace, which had been heated seven times hotter to make an example of them. However, the king didn't know that an example was to be made for him by the King of all kings. The three Hebrews fell helpless, powerless, and hopeless into the fire. But they didn't stay down. They met the King of all kings who loosed them and raised them up, walking around with them in the midst of the fire. Who does that? Who ever heard of such a thing? King Nebuchadnezzar was astonished at the sight, and now persecution was turned into promotion. The king saw that the fire had no power over them, and he realized that there was no other God who could deliver like this. When we are truly willing to die with Him, we will reign with Him.

Second Timothy 2:12 says that if we suffer with Him, we shall also reign with Him. Again, we have an adversary who is enraged, much like king Nebuchadnezzar was enraged with Shadrach, Meshach, and Abednego. We don't have to appease our adversary to get him to leave us alone. We have an Advocate who has defeated him and stripped him of his power over us, and we find this to be never more true than when we are in the midst of the fire.

"When you pass through the waters, I will be with you; and through the rivers, they shall not overflow you. When you walk through the fire, you shall not be burned, nor shall any flame scorch you" (Isa. 43:2). Notice that it says when, not if. God knows there are going to be troubled waters and fiery trials, and we are going to suffer. He has already planned for it. The Lord Jesus said, in John 16:33, that in the world we would have trouble, but He also said that we should be of good courage because He has overcome the world. What significance does that have for us? First of all, it lets us know that we are not exempt from trouble because we belong to Him. But it also tells us that we can overcome the trouble of this world by the same power that enabled Him to overcome it. This was the point of His coming into the world—to become like one of us, to live as one of us, but to be different than us. He was not a slave to sin and the lusts of this world, because He was not conceived in sin and He knew no sin. However, Hebrews 4:15 says that the Lord Jesus was tempted in all points like we are, but without giving in to the temptation to sin. He came to give us the same power He had, so that we can be as He was in this world (1 John 4:17).

First Peter 2:21 says, "For to this you were called, because Christ also suffered for us, leaving us an example, that you should follow His steps." The Lord Jesus is our example. We should not think it strange to suffer fiery trials, because God has already planned for these trials to give way to promotion. The Lord Jesus humbled Himself and became obedient to the worst kind of death. Imagine that—the best being treated as the worst in order that the worst might be saved and transformed into the best. It was all according to the Father's plan, because the Lord Jesus was willing to humble Himself and be obedient to the utmost degree, the Father highly exalted Him and gave Him the name which is above every name. When we are willing to follow in His steps, we will not stay under the hand of our adversary. We will be promoted by the hand of our Advocate, as First Peter 5:6 says, "Humble yourselves under the mighty hand of God, that He may exalt you [lift you up or promote you] in due time."

I don't know about you, but when I am suffering, **in due time** can seem like a **long time**. These are the times when I have nothing else to go on but my faith in God. Furthermore, James 1:2–4 says, "Count it all joy when you fall into various trials, knowing that the testing of your faith produces patience. But let patience have its perfect work, that you may be perfect and complete, lacking nothing." James says that we know God is at work in us when we experience trials. Our adversary may be at work, but our Advocate is too, and His work is the greater work, which will ultimately bring us "all joy." We will see the glory of God manifested in our lives, brought to a level of completeness and maturity, lacking nothing, because we have been willing to let God write the story that gave way to glory.

The apostle Paul says in First Corinthians 1:26–29, "For you see your calling, brethren, that not many wise according to the flesh, not many mighty, not many noble, are called. But God has chosen the foolish things of the world to put to shame the [so called] wise, and God has chosen the weak things of the world to put to shame the things which are mighty; and the base things of the world and the things which are despised God has chosen, and the things which are not, to bring to nothing the things that are, that no flesh should glory in His presence."

Second Corinthians 4:16–18 says, "Therefore we do not lose heart. Even though our outward man is perishing, yet the inward man is being renewed day by day. For our light affliction, which is but for a moment, is working for us a far more exceeding and eternal weight of glory, while we do not look at the things which are seen, but at the things which are not seen. For the things which are seen are temporary, but the things which are not seen are eternal."

Do not lose heart. We can be tempted to lose heart and give up when we're going through trials and sufferings. Thus, it is so important to know the word the apostle Paul is speaking here.

We should not lose heart because God is doing something in the midst of our suffering. God is at work on the inside of us, the part that is eternal, the inward man. So, even though my outward person may be perishing, going through trials and tribulations, we don't lose heart if we know it is only to make way for the inward man to be renewed each day. Our story, what we have suffered, will be turned to glory, by the One who is our glory.

Whatever we are going through, He calls us to examine ourselves. Look inside, as the apostle Paul says in Second Corinthians 13:5, to know how much we are in the faith. To know that the Lord Jesus is in us and with us and for us. This is the inner confidence of the inner man, and we don't gain that confidence without a test to prove our faith in a God who proves Himself faithful. Psalm 27:13 says, "I would have lost heart, unless I had believed that I would see the goodness of the Lord in the land of the living." Unless I had believed. This is how we obtain that belief.

It is easier to not lose heart if we realize that the Holy Spirit is at work through our affliction. Paul refers to it as a light affliction which is but for a moment. We might be tempted to think when we're going through it that it sure doesn't seem light and it certainly doesn't seem like just a moment. In fact, sometimes it seems like it's never going to end. However, in those times, we have to look at what God, our Advocate, is working for us compared to what our adversary is doing to us. Our Advocate may give him access to our outward man, which is going to pass anyway, and rightfully so, because it has been marred by sin which brings forth death. But our Advocate will never give our adversary access to our inner man or person, which has been freed from sin and death by His blood. And this is the far more exceeding and eternal weight of glory. What our adversary is doing is for but a moment compared to what our Advocate is doing, which is forever. This is what God is working, this is what we have to look forward to, and this is why we don't lose heart.

Several years after our son went to heaven following his bicycle accident, my wife had a dream about him. She said that in the dream they were together again, and they picked up right where they left off, as though they had only been apart for a moment. It was glorious. I believe that it was the Lord who gave her that dream to let us know that's how it's going to be for us who have the hope of eternal life. We'll be raised up and pick up right where we left off, the glory of it making the pain of it seem only momentary. And from that point on there shall be no more pain, and no more sorrow, and no more trouble, and no more suffering, and no more death. Hallelujah!

Another way to prevent losing heart is not to focus too long on what we're going through. Focus more on what we're getting to and going to. Not looking so much on the trouble I see, but more so fixing my attention on what I do not yet see. The trouble I see now is not going to last, but what I gain from going through it is going to last forever. The reward will be eternal life, with a new body that will never know sickness, sorrow, pain, or death. This troubled world is eventually going to give way to a new world under new heavens that will never be spoiled again by sin and death, where God will live together with His people forever as He always intended. We can come to realize that we will never again see the trouble we have known in this life.

I am reminded of another incident that occurred while Jeffrey was fighting for his life in Beth Israel Deaconess Hospital.

Our third born son, Jared, who had turned twenty-one the day of Jeffrey's accident, came up to me and said, "Dad, why is this happening to my brother? He's a Christian. He loves God. How can this be?"

In my natural state, I would've said, "I don't know." But at that moment, I believe the Lord gave me an answer.

I said to him, "Son, because things like this happen in this life, and we are not necessarily exempt from them because we are Christians. These things are part of the nature of this life and this world, but I guarantee you they will not be part of the life and the world to come, and that's where you've got to keep your focus, as painful as this is right now."

The only way we get through the trials and troubles of this world is by knowing there's a world to come where there will be no more suffering forever.

First Thessalonians 4:13 says that we don't grieve as those who have no hope. We have hope. The hope of resurrection, the hope of eternal life, the hope of the world to come. First Corinthians 15:19 says, "If in this life only we have hope in Christ, we are of all men the most pitiable." We can easily become discouraged and lose heart if we focus on this world. Where my treasure is, there my heart is. If my treasure is Jesus and eternal life with Him, I will never be disappointed, and there will be no losing heart. He promises that it is waiting for us, as He paid for it with His blood.

Hebrews 12:1 attests that we are surrounded by a great cloud of witnesses who have gone before us. Chapter eleven of Hebrews enumerates these witnesses. Noah prepared an ark when there was no rain. Abraham left his home not knowing where he was going because he already saw it with the eyes of faith and believed that God would lead him to it as he stepped out.

Moses refused to be called the son of Pharaoh's daughter, "esteeming the reproach of Christ greater riches than the treasures in Egypt" (Heb. 11:26). He was a foreshadowing of Christ who said in Matthew 5:12, "Rejoice and be exceedingly glad [when you are reproached and persecuted], for great is your reward in heaven, for so they persecuted the prophets who were before you." When we are heavenly minded, we live in heaven on earth.

Hebrews chapter eleven goes on to speak of Rahab, Gideon, Barak, Sampson, Jephthah, David, Samuel, the walls of Jericho coming down, and the prophets who through faith subdued kingdoms, worked righteousness, obtained promises, and stopped the mouths of lions. Our adversary, the devil, is like a roaring lion who seeks to intimidate us with trouble and tribulation, but he has been and will be silenced with a greater roar of our Advocate, the Lion of the tribe of Judah, the Lord Jesus!

Chapter eleven also speaks of others who had trials of mockings and scourgings, chains and imprisonment. They were stoned, sawed in two, slain with a sword, wandered about, destitute, afflicted, tormented. In heaven's estimation, the world was not worthy of them. These were the true warriors and gladiators of the faith who died without receiving the promises. Yet having seen them afar off, they embraced them and confessed that they were strangers and pilgrims upon this earth. Those who say such things declare plainly that they are looking elsewhere for a homeland. They desire a better, heavenly country. Therefore, God is not ashamed to be called their God. Those who have forsaken the love of this world, and the love of the pleasures of sin for a season, in favor of the love of the Father and His Son Jesus Christ forever, will bring no shame to God who has prepared a city for them.

In First Timothy 6:12, the apostle Paul exhorts Timothy to "fight the good fight of faith." The fight is called good because it has a good outcome—an ever-increasing faith in the Lord Jesus that won't quit in the face of adversity. Paul knew full well that faith was a fight. The Lord Jesus let him know that right from the beginning of his calling as Acts 9 recounts His words to Ananias, "For I will show him how many things he must suffer for My name's sake" (v. 16). Paul's adversity was his Advocate's university in which he would learn obedience and humility. God paved a way to authority and victory over all of the power of the adversary.

Second Timothy 3:12 states that all who desire to live godly lives will suffer persecution, and that's where the fight of faith comes in. We must understand that. The Lord Jesus told Peter in Luke 22:31, Satan, your adversary, has asked permission to sift you as wheat. The wheat sifting process begins with a sharp shaking to bring the chaff and straw to the surface. Next, the sieve is held in a slanting position and jerked up and down while blowing across the top of it with great force. Peter is about to experience a great shaking that is going to bring to the surface his true, fallible human nature which we all inherited from the first man, Adam. When Peter said he was willing to die with Him, the Lord Jesus told him that he would deny Him. The spirit is willing, but the flesh is weak. We can only prevail by the power of the Holy Spirit. However, in verse thirty-two, the Lord Jesus tells Peter, "I have prayed for you." Here the word you is plural because it was not just for him, but all the disciples of the Lord Jesus. He is letting us know that the sifting at our adversary's hands is inevitable, and will be permitted, because it is vital that our faith in Him be separated from everything else that would diminish it. Furthermore, it proves that our faith in Him can never be accomplished by human nature or willpower, but only by the power of the Holy Spirit. Peter was confident in his statement that he was ready to die with the Lord Jesus, if need be, but when it came right down to it he denied three times that he ever knew Him. After the third time, Peter went out and wept bitterly. If you have ever wept bitterly over your failure to have faith in the Lord Jesus in the face of adversity, recognize that God has designed this adversity to bring to the surface any self-reliance or self-confidence we have and to bring us into complete reliance upon Him. It is beautiful and comforting to see the transformation in Peter after he is filled with the power of the Holy Spirit, as he states in his first letter to the church, "Though now for a little while, if need be, you have been grieved by various trials, that the genuineness of your faith, being much more precious than gold that perishes, though it is tested by fire, may be found to praise, honor, and glory at the revelation of Jesus Christ" (1:6–7).

It is no wonder that the apostle Paul refers to our faith in Christ Jesus as a good fight. Faith is not just a walk in the park on a sunny day when everything is going my way. Faith is a fight. It's a walk in the dark, when I can't see the forest for the trees, when I don't feel His presence. Faith is a fight when He doesn't seem to be helping me, when I feel like giving up, when I'm wondering if He's really there. Let's be honest, we could all be subject to such feelings, but that's where the fight of faith comes in. Genuine faith is developed in the fight; not just fair-weather faith, bad-weather faith, any kind of weather faith. Genuine faith is cultivated when I have no one else to lean on but God. I discover that when I'm being sifted, doubt, fear, and anxiety can rise up and challenge my faith in God. However, by the power and help of the Holy Spirit, we engage in the fight and say to those feelings, "Get behind me, get out of my way, you are an offense to my faith in the Lord Jesus." Faith is a good fight. You can count on it, and the more we go on with God, the more intense the battles can get. However, if we are willing, the battles will only serve the purpose of making our faith in Him that much more intense. God will cause the adversity to work for us if our faith in him does not fail in the process.

The good news is that we are not fighting this good fight of faith alone. Our Advocate is fighting with us and for us. As He said to Peter, "But I have prayed for you, that your faith should not fail" (Luke 22:32). When the Lord Jesus prays for you, the Father listens to Him as He said in John 11:42, "I know that You always hear Me." As a matter fact, Our Advocate "always lives to make intercession for [us]" (Heb. 7:25). We can rest confidently in the fact that our Advocate is always praying for us, and the Father always hears Him; He will never let us down. He has sent the Holy Spirit to make good on that promise, and if God be for us, who can be against us?

If we go back to First Timothy 6:12, Paul goes on to say that we should take hold of eternal life. This is the ultimate good in the good fight of faith. This is what the Lord Jesus speaks of in John 10:10, "I have come that they may have life—" Eternal life, the life stolen from us by our adversary. Our adversary would like nothing more than to devour the life the Lord Jesus offers us. But we've got to lay hold of it.

> *Not that I have already attained, or am already perfected; but I press on, that I may lay hold of that for which Christ Jesus has also laid hold of me. Brethren, I do not count myself to have apprehended; but one thing I do, forgetting those things which are behind, and reaching forward to those things which are ahead. I press toward the goal for the prize of the upward call of God in Christ Jesus.*
>
> (Phil. 3:12–14)

We are continually pressing on, pressing in, going forward, not looking backward and getting stuck there. Our Advocate's direction is forward. He is by our side encouraging us to keep going forward. Conversely, our adversary is also there doing everything he can to remind us of the past to keep us from advancing the kingdom of God. Our Advocate has forgiven and forgotten our past failures, faults, and sins, and so should we. He is calling and leading us toward the prize of the upward call in Christ Jesus. Our adversary wants to drag us downward with him; our Advocate is ever drawing us upward with Him.

The Lord Jesus left the world He was never part of. He only came into this dying lower world to show us the glory of a never-ending upper world, and then to make the way for us to lay hold of it and enter into it through His death on the cross. The Lord Jesus did not come into the world to save the world. He came into the world to save us from the world that held us captive through sin and death.

Our going forward is a process of leaving this world behind us and pursuing the world ahead of us. In fact, we know that when we do actually leave this world through death, we are not taking anything or anyone with us. We are leaving it all behind. We came into this world with nothing, and we will leave with nothing. We are just passing through to eternity. However, where we spend eternity depends on whether we have laid hold of eternal life in Christ Jesus. Second Timothy 4:8 says, "Finally, there is laid up for me the crown of righteousness, which the Lord, the righteous Judge, will give to me on that Day, and not to me only but also to all who have loved His appearing." We live this life looking forward to the life to come, bringing as many to the knowledge of the Savior as He gives us.

The apostle Paul says to take hold of what you have confessed, the hope of eternal life. I submit to you that confession is the easy part. Possession of our confession is the harder part. That is where the fight comes in. That is where the pressing comes in, moving forward toward possession, laying hold of what we have confessed, living what we have confessed. Our adversary will do everything he can to prevent us from possessing what we're confessing. He is not afraid of our confession, but he trembles when we have laid hold of the One who crushed his head through the cross. So, we move forward, believing Him who has promised to finish in us what He finished on the cross by the power of the Holy Spirit.

Philippians 2:12–13 says, "Work out your own salvation with fear and trembling; for it is God who works in you both to will and to do for His good pleasure." Salvation and eternal life is a workout, and intended to be worked out by us, but through Him who lives in us. It's a joint venture. We work out what He works in. He establishes a faith in us that makes a willingness then to do what pleases Him. It's an inward motivation that leads to an outward manifestation. We are only living out what He has perfected in us as we continue to put our faith in Him. If there is no working in, there will be no working out. And so, we fight the good fight of faith in Christ Jesus and the Holy Spirit to move us ever forward toward eternal life.

Finally, let us return to the apostle Paul's second letter to the Corinthians, where he says, "Therefore most gladly I will rather boast in my infirmities, that the power of Christ may rest upon me" (12:9). In other words, "If that is going to be the outcome, then I will take it." The word infirmities means "weaknesses in body or mind, lack of strength, and feebleness of health or sickness."[12] The word rest means "to

---

[12] Strong, James. "769 ἀσθένεια (astheneia)," Strong's Greek: 769. ἀσθένεια (astheneia) (BibleHub, 2023), https://biblehub.com/greek/strongs/769.htm.

take possession of, to move in, to live in."[13] So, Paul is saying, "If that's how his power comes to me, I will most gladly bear the infirmities to receive the reward of His power." The reward is greater than the sacrifice; the benefit is greater than the cost.

Oftentimes, revelation comes by tribulation. When we've gone through an ordeal of suffering that crushes us, we get a revelation and a manifestation of His power that couldn't have come any other way. Our desperation and helplessness positioned us to receive His strength and power. Isaiah 40:29 says, "He gives power to the weak, and to those who have no might He increases strength." I know this because it's what His Word says, but I come to believe it when I am weak and find Him giving me strength over and above my weakness, proving His Word not only to be true, but true in me. So, even though our adversary may seek to render us powerless, he is only playing right into the hands of our Advocate to empower us to be more than conquerors through Him who loves us. I now know my Redeemer lives because when I was crushed and weak, His resurrection power came in and lifted me up. I didn't do it; I couldn't do it if I tried. He did it. As Paul says in verse ten, "when I am weak, then am I strong." So, we can come to place where we are actually glad to be made weak, because we have come to know that our weakness will be filled with His strength. Our Advocate can use our adversary to bring us to a place where we are

---

[13] Strong, James. "1981 ἐπισκηνόω (episkénoó)," Strong's Greek: 1981. ἐπισκηνόω (episkénoó) (BibleHub, 2023), https://biblehub.com/greek/strongs/1981.htm.

finished and have nothing left; it's all Him, His power moving us, strengthening us, lifting us above it all.

If we want the glory, there will be a story behind it, for there is no glory without a story. So take heart when God is writing your story, because the end of the story is to bear His glory and bring Him glory.

The Lord Jesus says in John 17:1, "Father, the hour has come. Glorify Your Son, that Your Son also may glorify You." The hour He's speaking of is the hour of His suffering and the glory that would follow. His story was the greatest story ever told, with the greatest glory that ever will be seen for all eternity. As His disciples, we have the honor of continuing to tell His story with our story and the glory to follow.

Chapter Four

Moses: Let My People Go!

God chose Moses to lead His people out of Egypt, where they had become enslaved to the Egyptians. Prior to their enslavement, they enjoyed great prosperity and abundance of food and material goods thanks to the leadership of Joseph and the favor he had with Pharaoh. Their numbers grew exceedingly, and all Egypt was filled with the people of God.

However, Joseph, his brothers, and all that generation died, allowing for a new king to reign over Egypt. This king did not know Joseph and was not so favorably disposed toward him. Has that ever been true in your life? You were enjoying blessing and abundance from the hand of your Advocate, and then the adversary comes in and the tables begin to turn. The favor you enjoyed begins to take a downturn.

At this writing, a grave example of such a turning is the COVID-19 pandemic that is sweeping much of the world with millions infected and hundreds of thousands losing their lives. If that were not enough of a downturn, millions more lost their jobs, businesses shut down, and millions lost their sense of well-being, waiting in food lines for the first time in their lives. A pandemic of fear was loosed upon the land as a result of the possibility of being infected with the virus and dying.

Americans were enjoying historic prosperity and unemployment rates and, just like that, everything turned upside down. Unemployment rates soared and prosperity hemorrhaged. Everything shut down. We could barely go outside our homes with state governments ordering us to stay home. There would be no more sports, no more concerts, no more church gatherings, no more shopping, no more going out to eat. There would only be the bare essentials: food and medical necessities. Even the toilet paper was all gone!

Revelation 12:12 says, "Woe to the inhabitants of the earth…for the devil [our adversary] has come down to you, having great wrath, because he knows that he has a short time." He has a short time before the return of the Lord Jesus, our Advocate. We have an adversary who hates the people of God, just as he hates the Lord Jesus. He would gladly rid the earth of us if he could, but he would rather rid them of their faith in the Lord Jesus. His real agenda is just that. If God permits him to kill me, God will raise me up, and my adversary can do no more. I'm home free from any further encounters with my adversary. However, my adversary's opposition and harassment are meant to discourage me and cause me to question the goodness of my Advocate.

He wants me to give up my faith in God. If he ever succeeds, then he has me for all eternity in everlasting torment. Christ, our Advocate, came into the world to save us from such a fate, and that is what the devil, our adversary, comes to steal, kill, and destroy. Our adversary will never succeed in his agenda with us as long as we continue to be mindful of his strategies.

Returning to the story of the Israelites in Egypt, the new king did not look favorably upon the children of Israel and became their adversary. We see in Exodus 1:11–14 that the Egyptians set cruel taskmasters over the children of Israel. The more they afflicted them, the more the children of Israel increased in number. This became a real threat to the Egyptians. Like our adversary, the Egyptians became pawns in the hand of God to make the Israelites more numerous. This is a marvelous principle throughout the Scriptures that we really need to understand when we are being afflicted. Our afflictions are ultimately going to turn out for our good by virtue of the pre-determined plan of our Advocate.

Psalm 34:19 says, "Many are the afflictions of the righteous, **but** the Lord delivers him out of them **all**." The more He does, the closer I draw to the Lord, the more my faith, confidence, and strength grows in Him, and the greater threat I become to my adversary. As long as I am willing, my adversary is not going to have his way. My Advocate is going to have His way, which is to give me power over the enemy. Again, this doesn't come magically, but through the battles and the victories, until we come to the "measure of the stature of the fullness of Christ" (Eph. 4:13). Isaiah 54:17 says that no weapon formed against me by my adversary is going to prosper, but my faith in my Advocate is going to prosper. His power in me is going to prosper.

As we saw in the last chapter concerning the apostle Paul, he was able to say, "most gladly I will rather boast in my infirmities [inflicted upon me by my adversary], that the power of Christ may rest upon me" (2 Cor. 12:9) In other words, if that is the result, then most gladly will I endure it, because the benefit is greater than the cost. What is important, however, is to keep my focus on that fact **when I'm going through the affliction**. This is what enables me to endure to the end. Let's take it a step further by the power of the Holy Spirit and do as James says in his letter to the church. "Count it all joy when you fall into various trials, knowing that the testing of your faith produces patience. But let patience have its perfect[ing] work, that you may be perfect[ed] and complete, lacking nothing" (1:2–4). I find it interesting that James starts his letter with this admonition, as though to say, "Expect it, but expect God to use it to perfect your faith in Him." The Lord Jesus endured the cross, despising the shame, because of the joy that was set before Him. He saw the end result, and the end result with our Advocate is joy unspeakable, full of glory, the glory of our God, which cannot be matched or defeated.

Such was the case for two sisters, Martha and Mary, who were devastated by the death of their brother, Lazarus, as recorded in the gospel of John, chapter eleven. They had sent for the Lord Jesus to come and heal him, but He didn't come when they sent for Him. When He did finally come, it was too late, as Lazarus had died in the meantime. "Lord, if You had been here, my brother would not have died" (John 11:21). The Lord Jesus calmly assures them that their brother will rise again. In other words, "I know this looks like the end, but it's not." Jesus said, "I am the resurrection and the life. He who believes in Me, though he may die, he shall live" (John 11:25). Whatever I am going through at the hand of my adversary is not going to end there. We will rise again, and again, and again, because we believe in our Advocate, the Lord Jesus, who is the Resurrection and the Life. He will raise us up by the power of His resurrection, and by the power of His might. We will know and testify of His greatness because He gave us the faith to believe it, and we have seen it. As the apostle John says in First John 1:3, "That which we have seen and heard we declare to you."

The apostle Paul, again, says in Rom. 5:3, "We also glory in tribulations." We have come to know that tribulation has a purpose from our Advocate's side. He uses the troubles of this world to produce in us endurance and a character that gives us hope for the future. The kind of hope expressed by Job in chapter 19:25–26, "I know that my Redeemer lives…that in my flesh I shall see God. It is the character of Christ described in Philippians 2:8, which says that He "humbled Himself and became obedient to the point of death, even the death of the cross." However, verse nine goes on to say, "Therefore, God also has highly exalted Him." When we are willing to humble ourselves before God during trouble, rather than shake our fist at God in anger, there is only one direction for us to go—up to newer and greater heights in God, with an ever-increasing assurance of the hope of eternal life.

As we return to the account of the children of Israel, we see that the more they were afflicted, the more they grew. Not only were the children of Israel subjected to cruel taskmasters, but their midwives were ordered to kill their infant sons. However, the midwives feared God more than they feared the consequences of disobeying the order—they saved the male children. The Bible says that all authority is established by God, and we should obey. Yet when that authority is exercised in direct violation to God's commands, we must obey God and entrust the consequences to Him. Such was the case when the Sanhedrin commanded Peter and John not to speak or teach in the name of Jesus (Acts 4:18). Their response was that the authorities could judge for themselves whether they should listen to them more than to God (Acts 4:19–20). When Pharaoh learned that the Hebrew sons were surviving, he ordered all his people to throw every newborn Hebrew son into the river (Ex. 1:22).

Moses was one of those sons. His mother hid him for three months until she could hide him no longer. She then made a floatable basket, put him in it, and put the basket in the reeds by the river's bank. Right from the beginning of

Moses's life, the adversary was out to kill him. Much like he worked through Herod to decree that all male children two years and under be put to death in order to kill the Christ-child, he was now using Pharaoh to do away with Moses. Later in Moses's life, he prophesied that God would raise up another Prophet like him, a deliverer, referring to the Lord Jesus. Once again, we see the connection between the Old and New Testament with the Old foreshadowing the New. As someone once said, "The Old is the New concealed; the New is the Old revealed."

The adversary was not able to succeed in killing Moses, for the Advocate intervened. Ironically, the Advocate used Pharaoh's daughter, who went down to the river to bathe and found the child in the basket, crying. She had compassion on him, knowing that he was a Hebrew child, and paid his mother to nurse him until he grew and became her own son.

Once again, the triumph of our Advocate over our adversary who would even seek to kill us. However, as we said, even if he is permitted to kill us, our Advocate will raise us up from the dead forevermore.

As an adult, Moses fled from Egypt to Midian after he killed an Egyptian who was beating a fellow Hebrew. He went from opulence to obscurity; from being the son of Pharaoh's daughter to tending his father-in-law's sheep on the far side of a desert. Nevertheless, God had him right where he wanted him. Though our adversary can trouble and attack us, our Advocate can use these attacks to put us right where He wants us. Time after time, our adversary plays right into the hands of our Advocate who works **all** things after the counsel of **His** will, **not** the will of our adversary. Though he may continue his efforts because he is blinded by his rage against us, the will of our adversary will never prevail. The Lord Jesus says in Matthew 16:18, "On this rock I will build My church, and the gates of [hell] will not prevail against it."

Moses is now on the back side of the desert tending sheep. Meanwhile, God has heard from heaven the groan of the children of Israel because of their cruel bondage at the hands of the Egyptians. He remembers His covenant with Abraham, Isaac, and Jacob that they would be exceedingly fruitful. God was moved with compassion toward his children. Even though our Advocate knows what He is going to bring out of our suffering, He is not indifferent toward it. Even though the Lord Jesus knew that He was going to raise Lazarus from the dead, He was not indifferent to the grief of the moment, and He **wept**. In fact, it is our pain that moves Him to cause us to reign with Him. Second Timothy 2:12 says that if we suffer, we will also reign with Him.

Exodus 3:2 says that the Angel of the Lord appeared to Moses in a flame of fire from the middle of a bush. It is significant to note here that the Angel of the Lord is capitalized. Other mentions of angels in the Scriptures are always lower case. This suggests that this is the Angel of all heaven through whom, as it says in John 1:3, "all things were made…and without Him nothing was made that was made." Most scholars agree that this is the pre-incarnate Son of God, the Lord Jesus Christ, who appears to Moses. The One of whom Moses, himself, speaks of in Deuteronomy 18:15: "The Lord your God will raise up for you a Prophet like me from your midst." Notice that the word Prophet is also capitalized.

As Moses draws near the bush to get a better look at this strange phenomenon, God calls his name twice, and says to him, "**I am** the God of your father—the God of Abraham, the God of Isaac, and the God of Jacob…I have surely seen the oppression of My people who are in Egypt, and have heard their cry because of their taskmasters [adversary], for I know their sorrows" (Ex. 3:6–7). God commissions Moses to work with Him to deliver His people from their cruel bondage to the Egyptians. Moses then poses the question to God, "When I come to the children of Israel and say to them, 'The God of your fathers has sent me to you,' and they say to me, 'What is His name?' what shall I say to them?" God said, "I AM WHO I AM…Thus you shall say to the children of Israel, 'I AM has sent me to you'" (3:13–14). In other words, "You can't reduce Me to a name that contains Me. You can't put Me in a box and have Me all figured out with your finite understanding. I am from everlasting to everlasting, without beginning and without end."

Let's return to the idea of the Angel of the Lord possibly being the pre-incarnate Lord Jesus. Two things stand out to me:

1. God says to Moses in Exodus 3:7, "I know their sorrows." This reminds me of Isaiah 53:3–4, "A Man of sorrows and acquainted with grief…surely He has borne our griefs and carried **our** sorrows."
2. Matthew 14:27 says, "But immediately Jesus spoke to them, saying, "Be of good cheer! It is I; do not be afraid." The Lord Jesus came to His disciples, walking on the water in the middle of the night. They were straining to maintain the stability of their boat in the middle of a sudden, fierce storm. They were dealing with adversity to the max! And now their Advocate is coming to them, but in a way, they don't recognize, in a way that is out of the natural order of things, and they cry out in fear, thinking they've seen a ghost. But He says, "Be of good cheer! It is I." In the original language, He is saying to them, "It is I am," which suggests that it is the same "I am" who appeared to Moses on the back side of the desert hundreds of years earlier.[14] Who else could come to them without a boat, walking on the water in the middle of the night, in the middle of a storm? Who else could command the wind and the waves and the storm to be

---

[14] Strong, James. "1510. εἰμί (eimi)," Strong's Greek: 1510. εἰμί (eimi) (BibleHub, 2023), https://biblehub.com/greek/1510.htm.

still? It's not natural; it's supernatural. And it wasn't a ghost, or a spirit. It was a man, the Man Christ Jesus, the God-Man who came down from heaven.

As noted previously, Moses was a type of Christ, as others were in the Old Testament. All the law and the prophets of the Old Testament pointed to the coming of the One who would fulfill all that was written in the law and spoken of Him by the prophets: the Son of God, the Christ, Jesus. Matthew 17:1–3 also gives further credence to this when the Lord Jesus takes Peter, James, and John to the top of a mountain where He is transfigured before them, "His face shone like the sun, and His clothes became as white as the light." And then Moses and Elijah, both of whom have long been gone from the earth, appear and begin talking with the Lord Jesus. It is no coincidence that these two men appeared to the Lord Jesus on that mountain top. Moses represented the law, and Elijah represented the prophets. Their discussion centered around the fact that Jesus was going to fulfill all that the law of Moses required and all that the prophets had spoken of Him. His three disciples saw and heard it all.

Yet, when God calls Moses from the burning bush, Moses questions whether the people will believe that God had appeared to him. In response, God empowers Moses to perform the miraculous—his rod turns into a snake and back again into a rod. His hand turns leprous and is restored. God gives him signs and wonders so that the people might believe this is God's man to lead them and deliver them from the cruel bondage of their adversaries, the Egyptian taskmasters.

Again, this foreshadows the coming of the Lord Jesus, who states in John 4:48 that unless the people see signs and wonders, they would not believe that He was the Son of God who came to deliver us from the cruel bondage of our adversary who held us captive to sin.

Moses packs up his family and moves to Egypt to confront Pharaoh. In Exodus 5:1, he tells Pharaoh that the Lord has said, "Let My people go!" First and foremost, they are God's people, and Moses is simply God's agent to let Pharaoh know that God is on the scene and demands the release of His people! This is the way we deal with our adversary: We tell him what God has said in His Word. The Word of God is the sword of the Spirit. We are not fighting by our words, our power, our name, or our authority, but in the name above every name, as it says in Philippians 2:9, the name of Jesus.

Jude verse nine says, "Yet Michael the archangel, in contending with the devil, when he disputed about the body of Moses, dared not bring against him a reviling accusation, but said, 'The Lord rebuke you!'" He did not stand on his own ground of authority in contending with the devil. He stood on the ground of authority of the One he served. We stand upon the ground of the victory of the cross of the Lord Jesus, our identification with Him as our Advocate, and the victory He has won for us over our adversary. Where do we get such confidence? From our knowledge of the Word of God and our faith in it, inspired and empowered by the Holy Spirit.

The apostle Paul prays this great prayer in Ephesians 1:17–21 for those with faith in the Lord Jesus:

> *That the God of our Lord Jesus Christ, the Father of glory, may give to you the spirit of wisdom and revelation in the **knowledge of Him**, the eyes of your understanding being enlightened; that you may **know**…what is the exceeding greatness of His power toward us [and for us] who **believe**, according to the working of **His mighty power** which He worked in Christ when He raised Him from the dead and seated Him at His right hand in the heavenly places, **far above all** principality and power and might and dominion, and every name that is named.*

Our Advocate wants us to know the greatness of His power. The more revelational knowledge we have of His Word, and the more faith we have in it, the less we will fear our adversary. Regardless of the weapon he forms against us, Isaiah 54:17 says it shall not prosper! God will see to it because we believe it. On our own, we are no match for our adversary, but he is no match for our Advocate, and we stand with Him. However, as we will see, our adversary does not just go away, but resists. As Pharaoh says to Moses and Aaron in Exodus 5:2, "Who is the Lord, that I should obey His voice to let Israel go?"

We should know that our adversary is going to challenge our knowledge of the greatness of our Advocate over him. Our adversary is going to continue to be our adversary and to be resistant. He is trying to scare us off, doubting the greater power of resistance we have because, "He who is in [us] is greater than he who is in the world" (1 John 4:4). Our Advocate encourages us to keep believing and trusting in His power of resistance in us until the adversary must flee. If we stand on the Word of God, our Advocate will turn the tables on our adversary, and it will not be us running from him, but him running from us. The Blessed Holy Spirit is in us and fights our battles with us to give us the victory.

Not only did Pharaoh resist Moses's demand, but he made it worse for the children of Israel, increasing their workload while decreasing Egyptian assistance by making them gather their own straw to make the bricks. Have you ever found that things can get worse when you're fighting the good fight of faith? Our faith fight makes our adversary angry because he does not want to "let us go." However, we need to know that the greater the battle, the greater the victory—the greater our faith and confidence in God becomes. This is the way it works in this fallen world ruled by the prince of the power of the air. Thank God his time is short, and his end is sure, but until then, we march on under the banner of the victory of our Lord Jesus.

The children of Israel confront Moses in Exodus 5:21. "You have made us abhorrent in the sight of Pharaoh and in the sight of his servants, to put a sword in their hand to kill us." Moses, in turn, questions the Lord, "Why have you brought trouble on this people?" (v. 22) I can imagine Moses thinking, "You sent me here to deliver Your people, and they are not being delivered. In fact, it's getting worse." You might say the same thing. You're doing what God wants you to do, standing on His Word, and circumstances are getting worse. We must understand that we have an adversary that continues to oppose and resist. As long as we fight with our Advocate on our side, the greater the resistance, the greater the victory. We will become, as Romans 8:37 says, "more than conquerors through Him who loved us." We don't get to be a conqueror without something to conquer. God is building us up in the spiritual, the way that weightlifting builds up our physical body. I'm not crazy about the rigors of lifting weights, but I have come to greatly appreciate the benefits. The greater the weight, the greater the resistance, but as we continue to push through the resistance, we are building up our strength to push through greater amounts of resistance. The greater resistance we encounter from our adversary, the greater the strength of our faith in our Advocate. We are no longer those of little or under-developed faith. God is developing our faith to the point of being fully confident in Him to overcome every challenge of our adversary.

We see this as we go on to Exodus 6:1, where God says to Moses, "Now you shall see what I will do to Pharaoh." Now I've got him where I want him, and I've got you where I want you, to make you a believer in Me and My greatness for My glory and your good. When God does a work, He does a complete work, not halfway. He's just getting started with me and my adversary. This is nowhere near being over, but when it is, I will be the man God intends me to be, walking in His authority over the adversary and seeing him crushed under our feet (Rom. 16:20).

The work is progressive as Exodus 23:30 says, "Little by little I will drive [the adversaries] out from before you, until you have increased, and you inherit the land." Returning to Exodus 6, in verse 3 God continues to speak to Moses, "I appeared to Abraham, to Isaac, and to Jacob, as God Almighty, but by My name Lord I was not known to them." The Hebrew word for Lord is Yhvh (Yahweh),[15] the God who is enough, the all-powerful One, the all-sufficient One. This hearkens back to what God told Moses at the burning bush, "I am that I am. I am what you need Me to be when you need Me to be it." The Lord is the fountain of being, blessedness, and infinite perfection. The apostle Paul says in Acts 17:28, "In Him we live and move and have our being." The name Yahweh became so revered among the Jews that they would not consider themselves worthy to even utter the name.

If we study Exodus 6:3 more closely and compare it with other verses, such as Genesis 15:1, 22:14, and 22:16, we can see that the patriarchs did know Him by the name Yahweh. This verse should be read more as a question than a

---

[15] Strong, James. "3068 יְהֹוָה (Yhvh)," Strong's Hebrew: 3068. יְהֹוָה (Yhvh) (BibleHub, 2023), https://biblehub.com/hebrew/3068.htm.

statement. "And by My name Jehovah, was I not known unto them?" They knew the name, but they had never seen the power of it that Moses was about to see. There was never the occasion for it because they weren't ready until now.

The same can be true for us. In the beginning of our journey with the Lord, we know His name and confess His name, but we do not yet know the full power of His name. Just as a child is not yet ready for the demands of adulthood, but they have within them the potential for it when they are prepared. As we go on with the Lord, it is a matter of progressive revelation of who He is and how great He is as He takes us through more advanced occasions for the need of His greatness. Our Advocate uses the opposition of our adversary whose intention is harm, but His intention is for our good.

In the apostle Paul's prayer for the church in Ephesians 1:17–23, he speaks to this very point. He prays for a "spirit of wisdom and revelation in the knowledge of Him…what is the exceeding greatness of His power toward us [and for us] who believe, according to the working of His mighty power." It is our Advocate's desire to reveal and to demonstrate that He is all-powerful. The working out of His power in our lives enables us to overcome all that our adversary would work against us. We often quote Romans 8:31, "If God is for us, who can be against us?" How do we really come to know that God is for us if there is nothing or no one against us? God's purpose of allowing our adversary to be against us is to demonstrate that He is for us. Our Advocate will overrule and overpower him and cause the adversity to work for us.

Christ is seated at the right hand of the throne of God, far above **all** rule, authority, power, and dominion. As we go on with Him, trusting Him, believing Him, we will see the working of His mighty power.

This is what Moses is about to see. The patriarchs heard of it, but they did not see it. It was not for them to see. Abraham and Sarah got a glimpse of it with the miraculous birth of Isaac, but God's primary purpose at that time was to establish them as His people. God's initial purpose is to establish us as His, belonging to Him, loving Him more than anything in the world, willing to lose our lives to gain His, being crucified with Christ (Gal. 2:20), and this doesn't happen overnight. This work that God is doing in us is an ongoing process as long as we live in these bodies of flesh. As Philippians 1:6 says, "He who has begun a good work in you will complete it until the day of Jesus Christ." When we meet Him face-to-face the work will be finished! God started it, and he will finish it as long as we don't give up.

For the apostle Paul, this work was daily, as he states in First Corinthians 15:31. He was ready to face death, if need be, for his identification and devotion to Christ, which he ultimately did when he was beheaded. On a daily basis, he died to himself and to his will and desires, in order to live unto Christ. Dying daily became a settled matter for him. This is true for us until it becomes a settled matter for us. Again, establishing a settled pattern of dying daily to my will and desires doesn't happen overnight, but I believe it is crucial if we are going to become true followers of the Lord Jesus. He says in Luke 14:27, "Whoever does not bear his cross and come after Me cannot be My disciple." The cross represents death to this world. No longer am I living for the pleasures of this world—more money, bigger house, and all the material goods I can accumulate. The Lord Jesus said to His disciples in Mark 8:36, "For what will it profit a man if he gains the whole world, and loses his own soul?" This world is passing away. Why would I want to live for a dying world? I would rather die for a living Christ who lives forever.

The people of God had borne their "cross" as slaves in Egypt for generations, and now it was time for them to know the greatness of His power revealed through Moses, who bore a cross of obscurity on the back side of a desert for forty years. This was in stark contrast to the place of prominence he held as the son of Pharaoh's daughter, believing he would be a ruler over his own people. God directs Moses and his brother Aaron to go to Pharaoh and tell him to let their people leave the land. He warns them that He's going to harden Pharaoh's heart, making him uncooperative. Why would God do that? The harder Pharaoh is in his resistance, the greater the judgments of God will be, and God's greater glory will be witnessed by his people. How often have we desired to see the glory of God only to discover that it comes on the heels of suffering? The apostle Paul says in Romans 8:18 that when he adds it all up, his conclusion is "that the sufferings of this present time are not worthy to be compared with the glory which shall be revealed in us." When God allows us to suffer, the glory to follow will be greater than the suffering before it.

Our adversary is not going to be cooperative when we engage him by the authority of Jesus's name. However, his lack of cooperation is the occasion for a progressively greater demonstration of the authoritative power of God within His disciples. First John 4:4 says, "He who is in you is greater than he who is in the world." The greater the resistance of our adversary, the greater the power of our Advocate. The power of the resistance of our adversary will never be greater than the power of our Advocate. We should not give in to discouragement when the resistance of our adversary increases. Our Advocate is using it to develop perseverance in us which, according to Romans 5:4, will then produce God-approved character. At the same time, we will see a demonstration of the superiority of our Advocate over our adversary. We gain a greater knowledge of the power of our Advocate because we've seen it, which reinforces our faith in Him and the veracity of His Word. First John 1:1–2 says, "That which was from the beginning, which we have **heard**, which we have **seen** with our eyes…concerning the Word of life—the life was **manifested**, and we have **seen**, and bear witness, and declare to you that eternal life which was with the Father and was **manifested** to us."

A witness is someone who has seen something, not just said something. Our Advocate uses our adversary to make us "eyewitnesses" of His power and superiority over our adversary. This enables us to declare with solid certainty that our Advocate is truly who He says He is and does what He says He can do.

God's judgements against the adversary, Pharaoh, and the Egyptians begin. Their river is turned to blood, the fish die, the river stinks, and they can't drink from it, but Pharaoh refuses to let them go. And so, God releases frogs—frogs everywhere, in their houses, their bedrooms, their baking ovens, and their kneading bowls.

This time Pharaoh promises to let them go if they get rid of the frogs. And so, Moses cries out to the Lord to rid them of the frogs, and the Lord complies. However, when Pharaoh saw that there was relief, he hardened his heart and would not let them go. This proved that Pharaoh was not promising complicity because he had reverence for God, he was only complicit to get rid of the frogs. Once the frogs were gone, he was no longer complicit. God is to be glorified and revered as God, and our reverence for Him alone is first and foremost. Our Advocate will use our adversary to prove that we are complicit to Him and His will for His glory's sake and not merely for our convenience. He is proving that we love Him for who He is, not just to get rid of the frogs in our lives and the adversary off our backs.

God then releases lice on the people and the livestock through the hand of Moses and Aaron. This time even Pharaoh's magicians, who had replicated the other two plagues, cannot replicate this one. They proclaim to Pharaoh that this was the "finger of God." Our Advocate doesn't have to use His whole hand, just the use of His finger will be enough! The Roman centurion said to the Lord Jesus in Matthew 8:8, "Only speak a word, and my servant will be healed." Pharaoh, however, still refuses to let the people go.

The plagues continue with flies, diseased livestock, destructive hail, locusts, and darkness over the land of Egypt for three days—darkness that could be **felt**. Despite these plagues, Pharaoh still refused to let the people go. And so, God plagues Egypt a tenth time, and He lets Moses know that this one will do it. This time Pharaoh will let His people go, because this plague will cost him and all of Egypt their first-born children and all the first-born of their animals.

> *And it came to pass at midnight that the Lord struck all the firstborn in the land of Egypt, from the firstborn of Pharaoh who sat on his throne to the firstborn of the captive who was in the dungeon, and all the firstborn of livestock. So Pharaoh rose in the night, he, all his servants, and all the Egyptians; and there was a great cry in Egypt, for there was not a house where there was not one dead.*
>
> (Ex. 12:29–30)

However, the children of Israel were spared, and not one of any of their firstborn men, women, children, or animals died. The Lord passed over them when He saw the blood of lambs on their doorposts as they had been instructed. Following the instruction of the Lord and His Word should **never** be taken lightly because it could be a matter of life and death. This remarkable event was the initiation of the Passover that the Jewish people still celebrate to this day. First Corinthians 15:54–57 states that death has been swallowed up in victory, the sting of it removed, and the grave no longer victorious. Death can no longer hold us in the ground. God gives us the victory through our Passover Lamb, our Lord Jesus Christ.

As we return to Pharaoh, the adversary of the children of God, we see that this time he lets the people go with everything that was theirs, with the addition of articles of gold, silver, and clothing that they requested from the Egyptians. They went out from under the heavy hand of Pharaoh with great victory and celebration. However, according to Exodus 13:17, God did not lead them out in a closer, more direct route toward the land of Canaan, the land of promise, the land of milk and honey, lest when they see war they would be tempted to go back to Egypt. He knew they weren't ready for war, so He led them by another way, the way of the wilderness.

Sometimes we wonder why God leads us into the wilderness. What is going on? Why is God letting this happen? It's preparation for war. God knows there is going to be war. Our Advocate knows that we have an adversary who will do whatever he can to keep us from getting to the promised land. Acts 14:22 says, "We must through **many** tribulations enter the Kingdom of God." We are in boot camp, learning to fight the good fight of faith and to endure hardship as good soldiers of the Lord Jesus Christ. Our Advocate is teaching us that our sufficiency is of Him and not of ourselves. We cannot trust in ourselves, but God alone is our strength and our help. We are coming to an understanding that our fight is not with flesh and blood but with powers and principalities and spiritual wickedness in high places. Our Advocate is bringing us to a position of complete and utter dependence upon Him. Song of Solomon 8:5 says, "Who is this coming up from the wilderness, **leaning** upon her Beloved?" When we are in the wilderness, He is there with us, and we learn to lean on Him. In the wilderness, we have no one and nothing else to lean on. We come to know that we can count on Him and to truly understand how great is His faithfulness.

We can't learn this any other way. We must gain more than head knowledge. We have to gain life knowledge through trials and tribulations. During these times, God proves His faithfulness to us and ours to Him. When we find ourselves in hard places, we truly come to know whether God is who He says He is and whether we believe what we say we believe. Romans 5:3–4 says that tribulation produces perseverance and perseverance produces character, but the more accurate rendering is "approved character," or "proven character." This takes place in the wilderness. The Lord Jesus's character was proven in the wilderness when the Spirit drove Him there to be tempted of the devil. The devil found out that this truly was the Son of God. He couldn't be overtaken by the temptation to turn stones into bread after fasting for forty days, or to throw Himself down from the pinnacle of the temple without getting hurt, or to worship the devil in exchange for power over all the kingdoms of the world. This was truly the character of God that could not be bought. And it is this same character, the character of Christ, that is being formed in us in the wilderness.

The apostle Paul states in Galatians 4:19 that he is in labor pains until Christ is formed in us. The word formed in the Greek is morphoó (mor-fo'-o) which refers to an internal reality as opposed to an external façade.[16] It speaks of a change of character which involves the putting to death of my character, my will, my desires, my plans, and my way in order to give birth to His.

In John 16:21 the Lord Jesus says that a woman has sorrow when she's in labor, but that sorrow is turned to joy when the child is born. What has been internal, the life within, has now come forth, and is now made manifest. It is now the words and deeds of Christ made visible in our lives to our great joy. All the pain, anguish, and bewilderment of the wilderness has been worth it in order to see Jesus. And when we see Him, we shall be like Him, and others will then see Him through us. We will be clothed with His likeness, His power, His peace, His joy, His righteousness, and His presence to share with those around us wherever we go. The

---

[16] Strong, James. "3445 μορφόω (morphoó)," Strong's Greek: 3445. μορφόω (morphoó) (BibleHub, 2023), https://biblehub.com/greek/3445.htm.

beautiful fragrance of Christ will go out from us and attract others to Him.

God is with His people in the wilderness, and He demonstrates it visibly. Exodus 13:21–22 says, "And the Lord went before them by day in a pillar of cloud to lead the way, and by night in a pillar of fire to give them light, so as to go by day and night. He did not take away the pillar of cloud by day or the pillar of fire by night from before the people." The Lord's presence manifested as a pillar of cloud in the daytime, and a pillar of fire in the nighttime. How comforting it is to know that He is with us day and night. As it says in Psalm 121, He who keeps us **never** sleeps, but day and night watches over us.

Next, we get to the good part, although initially it looks like a really bad part. Our journey with the Lord may start out looking like something bad, but He turns it into something good. Once again, to the great consternation of His people, God hardens the heart of Pharaoh and the Egyptians as reflected by their words in Exodus 14:5, "Why have we done this, that we have let Israel go from serving us?" And Pharaoh and his army pursued the people of God, overtook them, and cornered them—the Red Sea behind them and the Egyptians in front of them. Why would God let that happen after all the plagues and His heavy hand upon the Egyptians? He wasn't finished with them yet. What the Israelites don't know is that He is about to finish the Egyptians off once and for all. This is critical for us to know when we have experienced great victory by the hand of our Advocate only to see it followed by an even fiercer attack by our adversary. Why would God let that happen? Because He's about to finish off our adversary in this particular battle. This will result in us having increased authority over him. If we are willing, each subsequent battle will have the same result until He increases us to the point where we are reigning together with Him.

In verse four of Exodus 14, the Lord says that "I will gain honor over Pharaoh…that the Egyptians may know that I am the Lord." He's going to show them who's boss. We have often quoted the first part of Psalm 46:10 without quoting the rest of it. "Be still and know that I am God; I will be exalted among the nations, I will be exalted in the earth!" Most of the time we quote it as though God is speaking to us, but when you read the rest, and the verses prior, it is more likely He is speaking to our enemies. He is going to gain honor in the presence of our enemies. He is telling them to be still, be quiet, shut up, and to know that He is God defending us. In other words, "Back off! These are My people." This may have the effect of causing us to be still knowing that He is our defender, but He is not likely speaking to us, as much as He is speaking for us.

Returning to Exodus chapter 14, listen to what His people say to Moses in response to what is happening. In essence, "Did you bring us out here to die? We told you to let us alone and let us stay in Egypt and serve the Egyptians rather than die here in this wilderness." It didn't take long for them to forget how miserable they were under the heavy hand of their adversary. The same can be true for us when we are delivered by the grace of God from the life we were living and surrender to Him only to discover that His way may be through the wilderness. We are no longer slaves of our adversary, but we are now his enemies to be pursued, but not outside of the oversight and purposes of our Advocate.

Moses responds to the people's fear in verse thirteen, "Do not be afraid. Stand still, and see the salvation of the Lord." They are now going to personally witness the greatness of Yahweh. They are now going to see that if He is for them, none can be against them. God is fighting for them, and Moses tells them that when God is done, "the Egyptians whom you see today, you shall see again no more forever." Hallelujah! God wants us to have a personal witness of His greatness, and the only way you get a personal witness is with a personal battle wherein God demonstrates His greatness on your behalf so that your testimony has first-hand evidence. The apostle Paul says in Second Timothy 1:12, "For this reason I also suffer these things; nevertheless, I am not ashamed, for I know [I am personally acquainted with Him] whom I have believed."

We now understand that God hardened Pharaoh's heart to bring him out for the final victory. No longer would he have authority or rule over them again. When God allows our adversary to be hardened against us, with our backs against the wall, we need to not be afraid. Instead, stand still, resist him, and know that our Advocate is bringing him out to take him out. First Peter 5:10 says, "But may the God of all grace, who called us to His eternal glory by Christ Jesus, after you have suffered a while, **perfect, establish, strengthen,** and **settle** you." His authority is perfected, strengthened, established, and settled in us as we are willing to humble ourselves under His mighty hand. From personal experience, we come to know what authority Christ Jesus won for us on the cross.

The hearts of the Jewish leaders were hardened against the Lord Jesus, and they, in turn, were agents to harden the hearts of the people against Him as they cried, "Crucify Him! Crucify Him!" However, as it says in Acts 4:28, they only did what God the Father, had determined **beforehand** that they should do. He knew the adversary would incite the people to crucify the Lord Jesus. He had already planned for it. Otherwise, He would have never permitted it. There is nothing in our lives that God permits to touch us that He has not already planned for. Our adversary's hatred for God and His Christ has blinded him and thus sealed his own doom forever.

The keys of hell and death were stripped from him. His authority over us was abolished, as God said it would be from the very beginning after the serpent tricked the woman into eating from the forbidden tree. Adam and Eve disobeyed the command of God, and thereby, surrendered His delegated authority to the adversary. God let the adversary do it, but He wouldn't let him get away with it. The Seed, Jesus Christ, would come and crush his head, or headship over us. This is so important to remember when evil seems to be triumphing and good is losing ground.

Take the following verses, from Psalm 73:

But as for me, my feet had almost stumbled;
My steps had nearly slipped.
For I was envious of the boastful,
When I saw the prosperity of the wicked.
(v. 2–3)

They scoff and speak wickedly concerning oppression;
They speak loftily.
They set their mouth against the heavens,
And their tongue walks through the earth.
(v. 8–9)

And they say, "How does God know?
And is there knowledge in the Most High?
|(v. 11)

Surely, I have cleansed my heart in vain,
And washed my hands in innocence.
For all day long I have been plagued,
And chastened every morning.
(v. 13–14)

When I thought how to understand this,
It was too painful for me—
Until I went into the sanctuary of God;
Then I understood their end.
Surely You set them in slippery places;
You cast them down to destruction.

> *Oh, how they are brought to desolation,*
> *as in a moment!*
> (v. 16–19)

And we know the rest of the story. Moses stretched out his hand over the Red Sea, and the Lord caused the sea to be parted in the middle with a strong east wind all night until it was dry land for the children of Israel to pass through. Moses didn't do it; he just did what God told him to do: "Lift up your rod, and stretch out your hand over the sea and divide it" (Ex. 14:16). Moses believed God and proved it by obeying His command. He could have said, "That's ridiculous. Who ever heard of such a thing?" But he had seen the hand of God and was persuaded that God was able to do exceedingly, abundantly beyond what he could even imagine (Eph. 3:20).

The children of God walked right through the Red Sea on dry ground with the Egyptians in hot pursuit. God intervened yet again, causing the Egyptian chariots to get stuck in the mud, hindering their pursuit of God's people. Once they crossed, God commanded Moses to stretch out his hand over the walled-up waters of the Red Sea so that they crashed back over the dry land with the Egyptians in the middle of it. God brought the Egyptians out, initially, to the great dismay and terror of His people. But in the end, He took them out. Exodus 14:31, "Thus Israel saw the great work which the Lord had done in Egypt; so the people feared the Lord, and believed the Lord and His servant Moses."

We may suffer great anguish and agony when our Advocate allows our adversary to unleash his fury against us. However, as we hold fast to our faith and trust in our Father and His Son, Jesus Christ, we will see the greatness of our God. Again, we can't see it if we have no need for it. When we do, our faith in Him will be raised to the level of not just knowing, but believing and walking in the truth that "greater is He who is in me, and for me, than he who is against me."

Chapter Five

David—A Man After God's Own Heart

So Samuel said to [Saul], "The Lord has torn the kingdom of Israel from you today, and has given it to a neighbor of yours, who is better than you."

(1 Sam. 15:28)

Saul was rejected as king of Israel because of his disobedience to the command of the Lord through His prophet, Samuel. In fact, it says in the last verse of this chapter (v. 35), that God regretted having made Saul king over Israel. We should never think that God does not have feelings. We were made in His image and likeness, and we have feelings. Even though God knew that Saul would fail, it was not His will that he should. Ezekiel 33:11 says that God takes no pleasure in the death (or failure or fall) of the wicked. So, again, we see by this that God, our Advocate, has feelings of pleasure and displeasure.

Saul's failure was his own will, as he was made in the image of God with the power to choose, and God regretted his choice, taking no pleasure in his fall.

As a result, God charged His prophet Samuel with the task of anointing another king over Israel. He sent him to the house of Jesse, who presented seven of his sons to come before Samuel for consideration from the oldest to the youngest. As soon as Samuel saw the appearance of the eldest, Eliab, he said, "This has got to be the one. He's head and shoulders over all the rest." However, the Lord corrected Samuel, letting him know that's not the criterion God uses for choosing a king. Man looks at the outward appearance, but God looks at the heart. How does the heart look? Is it right? Is it clean? Is it honest? Is it tender toward God? If God, our Advocate, is ever going to put us in a position of authority over our adversary, we are going to have to let Him search us and, as Psalm 139:23–24 says, "know my heart, try me…and see if there is any wicked way in me, and lead me in the way everlasting." This means that there may be times that our Advocate will break our hearts to know whether our motive for serving Him is pure. He can have His way with me, whatever that way is. My heart has been stripped of all pride, self-seeking, and deceit.

As good as they may have looked, none of Jesse's seven sons were chosen by the Lord. Apparently, God didn't see what He was looking for in their hearts. Samuel asked Jesse if he had any more sons. In fact, he did—his youngest son, whom Jesse did not think worthy to invite for consideration.

Samuel, who knew that God had sent him to the house of Jesse to anoint the next king of Israel, insisted that Jesse send for David. This was a matter of utmost importance.

When David arrived, the Lord said to Samuel, "Arise, anoint him; for this is the one!" (1 Sam. 16:12) Something was noticeably different about David. He was ruddy and good-looking, but he had strikingly bright or beautiful eyes. Matthew 6:22 says that the eye is the lamp of the body, or to paraphrase a well-known saying, "the window of the soul." This verse goes on to say that if the eye is good, we will be filled with light, or spiritually speaking, Godly perspective. Oftentimes, you can tell what's in a person's heart by looking into their eyes. According to First Samuel 13:14, quoted by the apostle Paul in Acts 13:22 in the New Testament, God saw that David was a man after God's own heart. One after God's own heart is one who **delights** to do all the will of God. Such a one is a God-pleaser, not a man(kind)-pleaser. He or she is one who goes after, who pursues the heart of God, to know the heart of God, and ultimately make His heart their heart. That is the definition of one who is after the heart of God. One whose will becomes one with the will of God; one whose desires become one with God's desires.

David was not worthy of consideration from the natural point of view. After all, he was a teenager tending his father's sheep. However, God saw his heart and knew he had the heart of a king. If our heart is right before God, we have the potential to become what God has made us for. For some, that can be kingly potential, no matter how things look at the moment. God is not so much impressed with our physical prowess or how talented or gifted we are. He is more interested in the quality of our hearts, because it is the quality of the heart that supports the gifts and talents and keeps them from swelling us with pride that leads to destruction. God is looking for a heart that He can have His way with, because His way is the way that leads to life. My way is the way that leads to death. God has no difficulty gifting me and empowering me. The bigger challenge is, can I completely surrender my heart and will and mind to Him?

> *Though I speak with the tongues of men and of angels, but have not love, I have become sounding brass or a clanging cymbal. And though I have the gift of prophecy, and understand all mysteries and all knowledge, and though I have all faith, so that I could remove mountains, but have not love, I am nothing. And though I bestow all my goods to feed the poor, and though I give my body to be burned, but have not love, it profits me nothing.*
>
> (1 Cor. 13:1–3)

It is not so much a matter of what I do as why I do it. My motivation must be love for God and for others.

David, a man after God's own heart, is chosen by God to be the next king over Israel and is anointed by Samuel. The Spirit of the Lord comes upon David at that time and remains upon him from that day forward. At the same time, the Spirit of the Lord departs from his predecessor, Saul, whose heart was after his own interests. The result of this dichotomy is that Saul becomes David's adversary despite the fact that they are of the same household, so to speak.

In Matthew 10:36 the Lord Jesus states that a person's enemies will be those of their own household. This was certainly true of Saul and David. It's not a matter of being of the same household, or bloodline, or tradition. It's a matter of being of the same heart toward God.

In Matthew 12:46–50, the Lord Jesus makes it very clear that His relatives (brother, sister, mother) are those who do the will of His Father.

Though David is anointed as the next king of Israel, it will be some time before he takes the throne. As is often the case, there will be a period of time between the calling and the commissioning. This will usually be a time of preparation, during which God prepares us for His purpose. In First Samuel 16:18, David is described as "a mighty man of valor, a man of war." David is being prepared as Israel's war king to battle Israel's adversaries. If we are going to be more than conquerors, our Advocate will schedule some battles for us at the hand of our adversary. How can we be conquerors if there is nothing to conquer? How can we be overcomers if there is nothing to overcome? How can we know victory if there are no battles?

God knows there will be battles because He knows we have an adversary. In fact, He knew every day of our lives before any one of them came to pass, according to Psalm 139:16, and there is nothing in our lives He hasn't already planned for. Israel's adversaries were physical armies, whereas our adversaries and our battles are spiritual. They may come in a variety of physical manifestations—trouble, tragedy, conflict, sickness, or loss, to name a few. Behind them is our adversary who seeks whom he may devour, and he seeks to devour our faith in our Advocate. He knows that if he kills us, he can't do anything more. He has no more opportunities to kill our faith and take us into the lake of fire with him for all eternity. This is why the apostle Paul said that he had kept the faith in spite of all the adversary's attempts to devour it with a long list of trials and tribulations. He fought the good fight of faith by the power of the Holy Spirit living in him, the same Spirit who lived in his Advocate, the Lord Jesus Christ. Ephesians 6:12 says that we don't fight with flesh and blood, but our fight is with principalities, powers, and rulers of the darkness of this age. And with spiritual hosts or armies of wickedness in heavenly places, all of whom seek to devour our faith.

This is demonstrated in David's confrontation with Israel's adversary, the Philistines, and their champion, Goliath, shortly after David is anointed king. This champion was nine feet nine inches tall. He wore a bronze helmet on his head and a coat of armor that weighed 126 pounds. He carried bronze armor on his legs and a spear with a tip that weighed sixteen pounds, the equivalent of a sixteen-pound bowling ball. He could throw this with great accuracy. He was a seasoned man of war, having fought undefeated in many battles.

David, on the other hand, was a shepherd, never having fought in a battle. When his three oldest brothers saw and heard Goliath, they freaked out. They and the rest of the army of Israel ran from him, fearing for their lives. Fear is a primary weapon of our adversary, who is like a roaring lion trying to scare us into thinking that our Advocate will not save us.

It is precisely at those times that we need to pour out our fears to our Advocate, and then declare our faith in Him to deliver us, remembering that He has **already** won the victory for us on the cross. He sent the Holy Spirit to bring that victory to us which is the ground we stand upon in the heat of the battle. David says to Goliath in First Samuel 17:45–46, "You come to me with a sword, with a spear, and with a javelin. But I come to you in the name of the Lord of hosts, the God of the armies of Israel, whom you have defied. This day the Lord will deliver you into my hand…that all the earth may know that there is a God in Israel." The faith our Advocate has given us works together with His power to enable us to resist our adversary until he flees. We do the believing of it; God does the working of it.

David was not a full-grown man, not a seasoned warrior, or even invited to join in the battle. He was sent with some food for his brothers. Isn't it amazing how God can turn the smallest task into the biggest task? David was obedient to his father's directive to take food to his brothers. This is the secret to God turning small tasks into big ones—our faithfulness in the little things. It's not how big or small the tasks are, it's our faithfulness to God in them. When we prove to God our faithfulness to Him in the little things, He knows He can entrust us with bigger things. We will continue to be faithful to **Him**, and the big things will not give us a big head. David was willing to serve the Lord and be faithful to Him in tending his father's sheep, where no one saw him but God. Sometimes God will put us in a place where no one sees us but Him. Be willing to be faithful in that unseen place.

You may remember that Moses was on the backside of the desert in relative obscurity tending sheep for forty years before God called him to lead thousands people out of Egypt. God knew He could entrust Moses with this task. He'd been proven in the unseen place. Our heart should be after God, not after people. Our heart should be after the praise of God more than the praise of people. The key to David's heart was his willingness to obey God and remain under His authority. He not only had a willingness to be under God's direct authority, but a willingness to be under God's delegated authority. He tended his father's sheep and brought food to his brothers at his father's command. When we are willing to be **under** authority, God can entrust us **with** authority.

David ran to the army and greeted his brothers only to find that they were running from the Philistine giant. He couldn't believe that they were afraid of him. Did they forget Who was on their side? Did they forget Who their Champion was? Psalm 124:2–3 says,

> *"If it had not been the Lord who was
> on our side, When men rose up against us,
> They would have swallowed us alive."*

Verse six goes on to say, "Blessed be the Lord, who has not given us as prey to their teeth." In First Samuel 17:26, David reminds them Who is on their side. "Who is this uncircumcised Philistine, that he should defy the armies of the living God?" (Circumcision was the sign that God gave Abraham to mark His people and to show that they were under His covering).

When David's oldest brother, Eliab, heard David his anger was aroused against him. He said to him, in essence, "Who do you think you are coming here to the battle? You're just a shepherd; you don't belong here; you don't know anything about this. Go back and look after those few sheep you left in the wilderness" (1 Sam. 17:28). This is another reminder of the fact that our ways are not God's ways. He defies conventional wisdom with heavenly wisdom so that He is the only one who can take credit for it. Otherwise, He would be no greater than us humans with our limitations.

> *For you see your calling, brethren, that not many
> wise according to the flesh, not many mighty, not
> many noble, are called. But God has chosen the
> foolish things of the world to put to shame the*

[so-called] wise, and God has chosen the weak things of the world to put to shame the things which are [considered] mighty, and the base things of the world and the things which are despised God has chosen, and the things which are not [worthless], to bring to nothing the things that are [considered worthy], that no flesh should glory in His presence.

(1 Cor. 1:26–29)

Verse 31 says that we should glory in the Lord. This is the very purpose for which He made us—His glory and His pleasure. We did not make ourselves so that we could say, "Look what I did!" God made us, which causes us to say, "Look what the Lord has done!"

Returning to First Samuel 17, David is brought before King Saul and lets him know that he will go and fight this Philistine giant. However, Saul's response lays out the odds against David's gesture in verse 33. "You are a youth, and he [Goliath] a man of war from his youth." What Saul didn't know was that David had experienced the mighty hand of God in the wilderness. We might wonder why we must go through the wilderness times in our lives. I believe it is during those times, when we have no other resources, that we learn dependence upon God. He gives power to the weak and helps the helpless. If we are ever going to be vessels of His power in the public place, we've got to know it first in the secret place, alone with our Advocate.

David understood this. He might not have had experience fighting with battle-seasoned champions of war, but he had experience fighting with lions and bears when they tried to steal sheep from his father's flock. He killed them with his bare hands! He says in verse 36, "This uncircumcised Philistine will be like one of them, seeing he has defied the armies of the living God." This was not about winning a war for the sake of the Israelites. This was about the honor of their God who was being dishonored. They would not have to worry about whether **they** could meet the challenge—their God would take up the challenge. God honors those who honor Him and guard His honor. When we are confronted with any challenge, trouble, or trial and we become fearful, we might want to look at it as defying the honor of God. David says in verse 37, "The Lord, who delivered me from the paw of the lion and from the paw of the bear, He will deliver me from the hand of this Philistine."

We must remember when we are under attack that the honor, glory, and integrity of our Advocate is being defied. We must take our stand and declare in faith, "How dare you defy the honor of our God to protect us, help us, and give us the victory. Now away with you fear, anxiety, and worry. Our faith is in our God." As it says in Second Corinthians 1:10, "Who delivered us from so great a death, and does deliver us; in whom we trust that He will still deliver us." We believe that our Advocate is able to deliver us, whether it be **from** the situation or in the situation, giving us the peace of God in the midst of the storm. Our

Advocate will take up the challenge as our desire is to align ourselves with His honor and glory. "God, be glorified when You are defied by my adversary." This is the heart of the issue, not so much the attack of our adversary, but the attack after the attack on our Advocate, taunting us with the foreboding thought that He's not going to deliver us. He's not big enough nor great enough. What we are facing is too big. And so, our adversary defies our Advocate's ability to protect and deliver us.

David was not intimidated by the stature or taunts of the giant. "Come to me, and I will give your flesh to the birds of the air and the beasts of the field" (1 Sam. 17:44). Now, look at David's response in verses 45–47.

> *Then David said to the Philistine, "You come to me with a sword, with a spear, and with a javelin. But I come to you in the name of the Lord of hosts, the God of the armies of Israel, whom you have defied. This day the Lord will deliver you into my hand, and I will strike you and take your head from you. And this day I will give the carcasses of the camp of the Philistines to the birds of the air and the wild beasts of the earth, that all the earth may know that there is a God in Israel. Then all this assembly shall know that the Lord does not save with sword and spear; for the battle is the Lord's, and He will give you into our hands."*

Mark Twain once said, "It's not the size of the dog in the fight, it's the size of the fight in the dog." There is no question that David is completely outmatched by the size and armor and skill of this giant. This is such an accurate depiction of how outmatched we are when facing our adversary. He is far more powerful and cunning than we are. Compared to him, we are like David with a sling and a bag of stones. However, David's confidence was not in his sling and stones. Philippians 3:3 says in part that we put no confidence in the flesh, or human efforts, to secure our salvation or to fight with our adversary. If we do, our adversary will easily give our flesh to "the birds of the air, and the beasts of the field."

David's confidence was in his God. The fight within David, the Lord of hosts, the God of the armies of Israel, was bigger than Goliath, and He was the ground for his confidence. The same is true for us. We stand upon the ground of our Advocate's victory through the cross. The Lion of the tribe of Judah has already confronted our adversary and won the battle with His blood. That is the ground upon which we stand when confronted by our adversary. We stand our ground in resistance to the adversary in the name of our Lord Jesus Christ, and by the power of His shed blood. James 4:7 says, "Resist the devil and he will flee from you." It doesn't say that you will flee from him, but the devil doesn't want you to know that. Verse 9 of Jude says, "Michael the archangel, in contending with the devil…dared not bring against him a reviling accusation, but said, 'The **Lord** rebuke you!'" It's not us who does the work, but Christ in us. Regarding the Lordship of Christ and the power of His Word, Revelation 12:11 says, "They overcame him [the adversary, the accuser of the brethren] by the blood of the Lamb and the word of their testimony."

The honor of David's God, his Advocate, is what is at stake here for David. He's not fighting for his own honor, as his brother Eliab accuses him in First Samuel 17:28. As David says later, "The Lord will deliver you into my hand…that all the earth may know that there is a God in Israel" (1 Sam. 17:46). Is this not the primary purpose of our life in Christ Jesus? That all the world would know that He is the Christ, the Son of the living God? He is the way, the truth, and the life, and no one can come to the Father, the one and only true God, but by the Lord Jesus, His beloved Son (John 14:6). No one can come to the Father on their own merit. All have sinned and fall short of the glory of God (Rom. 3:23). Only Christ Jesus, the Son of God, was sinless and hit the mark of the glory of God. Because of His sinless sacrifice, His blood can cleanse us so thoroughly that we can be as though we have never sinned! The Lord Jesus was willing to lay down His glorious life in exchange for our inglorious, sinful, unworthy life, so that we may come to the Father. Because of our faith in the Son of God, Jesus transfers His glorious, sinless life to us.

After the Lord Jesus was raised from the dead and just prior to His ascension back to the Father in heaven, He charged His disciples in Mark 16:15, "Go into all the world and preach the gospel to **every** creature."

However, we must come to terms with the fact that we will be confronted with strong opposition from our adversary as David was confronted by Goliath. If we are willing to stand by faith and contend for the honor and glory of our Advocate, we will find that it is only the occasion for our Advocate to display and reveal His majesty in the battle. For as David says, "the battle is the Lord's." When the battle is the Lord's, there will be victory. When I have a greater concern for my own welfare, I'm on my own. When my heart is fixed on the glory of God being revealed in the battle, the Lord, our Advocate, takes up the battle with us, and the victory comes. Then we have the opportunity to declare that there is a God in the church like none other who is able to make all of His enemies His footstool.

David did not see Goliath as **his** enemy, but the enemy of his God, and that's what motivated him. He was willing to engage in a confrontation in which the odds were against him. But again, he was not thinking of himself. He was thinking of his God who was being defied and dishonored, and that was intolerable for him.

When we are more concerned for how our Advocate can be glorified and honored in our situation, rather than just getting out of the situation, we can rest assured that our Advocate is going to show up and show off His glory. I believe the church of the Lord Jesus Christ would see a greater manifestation and demonstration of the glory of God if we had a greater concern for the glory of God than we do for ourselves. Revelation 12:11, mentioned above, continues with, "and they did not love their lives to the death." In other words, they had a greater concern for the glory of God than they did for their own lives. So many martyrs have been willing to give their lives for the testimony of Jesus.

I'm upset if I have a bad day or didn't get the job I wanted or the proper recognition. I've got a long way to go to get to the glory of God! An old chorus I used to sing is titled, "Let's Forget About **Ourselves**." If we can worship the Lord instead of ourselves, then we're going to begin to see what we've been longing to see—the glory of God revealed in the church in the form of signs, wonders, and miracles. These types of manifestations will bring many to faith in the Lord Jesus because our motive is purely for His glory. First Corinthians 10:31 says, "Whatever you do, do all to the glory of God." First Peter 4:11 says, "If anyone ministers, let him do it as with the ability which **God supplies**, that in **all things** God may be glorified through Jesus Christ, to whom belong the glory and the dominion forever and ever. Amen." There is no limit to what God will do when our primary motive is for His glory.

"So, David prevailed over the Philistine with a sling and a stone…but there was no sword in the hand of David" (1 Sam. 17:50). A sling and a stone were not conventional weapons of war. They were the weapons that God put into David's hand out in the obscure wilderness as he tended his father's sheep. Second Corinthians 10:4 says that the weapons He gives us are not conventional or man-made, but mighty in God for striking down the strongholds of our adversary. Some of these strongholds are worry, fear, anxiety, unrest, doubt, principalities, powers, rulers of the darkness of this age, and spiritual armies of wickedness in high places. Our battle is a spiritual one that requires engagement in spiritual warfare. It is not with people, but with the powers of darkness working through people. Therefore, the weapons with which we fight are weapons of prayer, worship, righteousness, the blood of the Lord Jesus, the power of the name of Jesus, the power of the Spirit, and the truth of the Word of God.

We learn to use these weapons in our wilderness times of trouble, when we're feeling outmatched and depleted of all our natural resources. In these times, we truly learn that He gives power to the weak, help to the helpless, and hope to the hopeless. How would we ever know this if we've never been weak or helpless or hopeless? None of us want to feel this way, but this is the training ground for our warfare. The more training we have, the more confidence we have in our Advocate, who is our personal trainer. Our faith in Him rises to new heights to fight new fights with spiritual weapons, rising to a new measure of authority until we reach the "measure of the stature of the fullness of Christ" (Eph. 4:13).

And so, David, the shepherd boy, is now becoming a man of war, a conqueror. King Saul set him over the men of war, and wherever King Saul sent him, he prospered. However, just that quickly, out of jealousy, King Saul turned from being David's advocate and became an adversary. When

David returned from his conquests, women danced and sang, "Saul has slain his thousands, and David his ten thousands" (1 Sam. 18:7). King Saul cast a suspicious eye upon David from that day forward. On the very next day, a distressing spirit from God came upon Saul and he prophesied inside the house. David was there and played his stringed instrument as he did at other times for King Saul. However, this time Saul had a spear in his hand and hurled it at David. David eluded the spear and escaped. First Samuel 18:12 says, "Saul was afraid of David, because the Lord was with him, but had departed from Saul."

This is very interesting to note. Our adversary, the devil, once the archangel Lucifer, who more than likely presided over the worship of God in the heavenlies, according to Ezekiel 28:13–15. Verse 17 continues, "Your heart was lifted up because of your beauty; you corrupted your wisdom for the sake of your splendor," suggesting that he let his beauty go to his head and made the very unwise choice to try to dethrone the God who made him. Isaiah 14:12–14 says, "How you are fallen from heaven, O Lucifer, son of the morning! How you are cut down to the ground…For you have said in your heart…'I will exalt my throne [my authority] above the stars of God…I will be like the Most High.'" Lucifer (which means day star), son of the morning, was cast down to the "ground," which very possibly was the yet unformed earth shrouded in darkness. He was no longer a son of the light, but the prince of darkness.

He is no longer Lucifer, the son of the morning, but Satan, the adversary, the prince of darkness. Our adversary, Satan, shared in the majesty of heaven and the throne of God until "iniquity was found in him." There was a hidden darkness in Lucifer, perhaps of jealousy over the praise given to God that he sought for himself, much like Saul over the greater praise given to David. That unconfessed darkness eventually drove Lucifer to try to overthrow the throne of God and put himself in the place of God. This is the true spirit of antichrist—not just being against Christ, but a dark desire to put oneself in the place of Christ. And so, the darkness in Lucifer has now overtaken the light that was once in him. He now presides over darkness, while fearing the Light that exposes and casts out the darkness. First Thessalonians 5:5 calls us children of the light. The Lord Jesus said that we who belong to Him are the light of the world and reflectors of His light. We are the light of truth that exposes what has been hidden in the darkness. The children of the Kingdom of Light are the greatest threat to the kingdom of darkness, so it should not surprise us when our adversary unleashes his fury against us.

Saul, from whom the light of the Spirit of the Lord had departed, was now taken captive by the darkness, and he feared David. We have one of two responses to fear: fight or flight. We either run away from what we fear or we attack what we fear. Saul's response to his fear of David was to attack him.

The same is true of our adversary. He fears the true children of light, those who have been enlightened with the truth of the victory of the cross and the blood of the Lamb. His response is the same as Saul's—to attack what he fears, to intimidate, accuse, threaten, and scare us. Yet our Advocate is faithful and makes a way of escape for us, according to First Corinthians 10:13. Furthermore, James 4:7 says that we should submit ourselves to God. When we do, we have the power of our Advocate working in us to resist our adversary until he flees from us. We will not run from him; he will run from us. Yet not us, but Christ in us.

David's adversary, Saul, continued his pursuit of David to kill him. Again, he tried to pin him against the wall with a spear and David escaped. Saul knew his days as king were numbered. Therefore, the evil spirit of the adversary drove him to kill David before Saul was dethroned, hoping to keep David from his God-ordained purpose. In the same respect, our adversary knows that his days are numbered. Revelation 12:12 tells us that he knows that he has but a short time. However, he is hell-bent on making the most of that short time. He is doing everything he can to attack and obstruct those who have a heart after God. So again, we should not be surprised or perplexed if we suffer opposition from our adversary, in whatever form that comes, when we pursue the purposes of our Advocate.

Time after time, God provided David a way of escape from the hand of Saul. God even went so far as to join the heart of Saul's son Jonathan with David as an advocate for him, enabling him to know what evil scheme Saul was plotting against David. The same is true for us with our adversary. Second Corinthians 2:11 says that we are not ignorant of our adversary's schemes against us. The Holy Spirit lives in us to guide, educate, teach, and train us in the warfare waged against us by the adversary. Through the Holy Spirit, we know that our adversary is a liar. We know that he is a deceiver. We know that he is an accuser, a murderer, and a roaring lion. We know that he even masquerades as an angel of light. And we know the difference between his voice and his ways, and the voice and ways of our Advocate. Such an example is found in Second Timothy 1:7, which says, "God has not given us a spirit of fear [fear doesn't come from our Advocate, it comes from our adversary], but of power and of love and of a sound mind."

God also gathered four hundred men around David to stand with him in his defense against the unwarranted, murderous pursuit of King Saul. It is interesting to note that First Samuel 22:2 gives a description of the men who aligned themselves with David. They were in distress, in debt, discontented or in bitterness of soul. Why would these kinds of men be drawn to David? I would suggest that it was because they saw in David what they saw in themselves, but something more. They saw in David a man who was not overcome by it, not defeated by it, not stopped by it, and they were willing to follow him as their captain to lead them out of their distress, out of their debt, out of their bitterness. We have such a Captain who came to lead us out of our distress, our indebtedness, and bitterness of soul. The Captain of our salvation. The One who was tempted in every way we would ever be tempted. The One who suffered more than anyone would ever suffer. The One who was well acquainted with grief and sorrow and pain. The One who was willing to become sick with our sicknesses and overcame it all for us. The Lord Jesus Christ, hallelujah!

As we are willing to go forward, trusting the Lord and wholly leaning on Him, He will bring us others to whom we can minister. Ultimately, we will be joined together as the army of the Lord, willing to wage war under the leadership of our great Captain, the Lord Jesus. In First Samuel 23:1–5, David inquired of the Lord when his supporters expressed their fear of fighting with the Philistines who were robbing the inhabitants of Keilah. As valuable as it is to have those who stand with you, we must never let them be the determining factor as to what we should do. We must then do what David did and "inquire of the Lord," and when he did, contrary to the advice of his supporters, the Lord told him to go. We will never truly know the greatness of our Advocate if we don't go, if we are paralyzed by fear and doubt. If I have to go afraid, then let me go afraid. Ultimately, my fear will leave me when I see the greatness of my Advocate slaying the giant that I feared. This serves to reinforce the fact that I didn't have to be afraid in the first place, and hopefully I will be less afraid the next time and the next time until I'm not afraid anymore. We won't know if we don't go! We must ask the Lord to give us the same spirit Queen Esther had when faced with the annihilation of her people. Speaking of her decision to ask for the intervention of the king, which was against the law, she said, "If I perish, I perish" (Est. 4:16). After praying and fasting for three days, asking others to join her in this, she took the plunge and saved her people.

Back to the example of David, First Samuel 23:14 says that Saul pursued David **every day**, but God did not deliver him into Saul's hand. Even if our adversary troubles us every day, our Advocate will not deliver us into his hand! Our adversary can only do what our Advocate permits him to do, and He will not permit him to take us captive. Our Advocate has the final word. Our Advocate is Lord over all!

Although Saul kept up his pursuit of David, he escaped from the hand of Saul time after time. David had occasions in which he could have killed Saul, even with the encouragement of his men, who concluded that the "Lord" had delivered Saul into his hand. However, David refused to do so because Saul was still the king anointed by God and he would not touch the Lord's anointed. He would not take matters into his own hands, but let God deal with Saul. The same is true in dealing with our adversary. We don't take him on and try to get tough with him; he's way "tougher" than we are. We do as the archangel Michael did in contending with the devil over the body of Moses, "The Lord rebuke you!" (Jude v. 9)

Finally, we see that David's Advocate, the Lord God Almighty, had already determined the end of his adversary,

Saul. First Samuel 31:1–5 tells us that Saul was severely wounded by the Philistines, who were determined to take him out. Saul ended up taking his own life before the Philistines could abuse him and then finish him off.

David refused to take vengeance on Saul, although he was unfairly and unjustly pursued by Saul for no other reason than fear and jealousy. Deuteronomy 32:35 says, "Vengeance is Mine, and recompense." The apostle Paul quotes this in Romans 12:19, when he writes, "Beloved, do not avenge yourselves, but rather give place to wrath; for it is written, 'Vengeance is Mine, I will repay,' says the Lord." Also, First Peter 2:23 says of the Lord Jesus that when He was (unjustly and unfairly) reviled, He did not retaliate, "but committed Himself to Him who judges righteously."

The same is true for us, particularly when our adversary directly, or indirectly through others, attacks us unjustly and unfairly. We commit ourselves to Him who judges justly. We dare not give in to the temptation to defend ourselves—that is our Advocate's realm. He will take up our case; He specializes in these cases.

As I stated in Chapter Three, in my days as a social worker I became the head of a non-profit agency. I described in that section how my employment with the agency was terminated through no fault of my own. As I drove home that day, I was stunned and shaken because I did not see this coming. However, the Lord did, and in fact spoke to me about it. He said, "This was not their doing, but My doing." It was my Advocate's time and His way to move me out of that job and into ministry. However, that was not the end of the story. Remember, we must commit ourselves to Him who judges justly, especially when we've been unjustly judged. Several years later, I received a phone call from a person who knew the individual who led the coup against me in that agency. This person informed me that the other individual had falsified records and their own qualifications in an attempt to get my position. This ultimately failed, but the real tragedy was that this man had now been missing for five days. I learned the next day that they found him in a wooded area in his car. He had shot himself to death. I shuddered to the very core of my being when I heard the news.

God has already determined the end of our adversary. Whenever he comes against us, we must remember on the authority of the Word of God that he is a defeated foe who will eventually be cast into the lake of fire. Until then, we commit ourselves to Him who judges justly.

Chapter Six

The Lord Jesus Christ— The Advocate

"We have an Advocate with the Father, Jesus Christ the Righteous."

First John 2:1

In the introduction to this book, we said that the Greek word for advocate was paraklétos (par-ak'-lay-tos). This word comes from pará, meaning "beside,"[17] and kaléō, which means "to call."[18] So, taken together, it means a calling to one's side, an intercessor, comforter, counselor.

In John 14:16, the Lord Jesus says that He will pray to the Father, and He will give us another Helper, an Advocate who will abide with us forever. In verse 17, the Lord Jesus goes on to say that not only will He be with us, but

---

[17] Strong, James. "3844 παρά (par-ah')," Strong's Greek: 3844. παρά (par-ah') (BibleHub, 2023), https://biblehub.com/greek/strongs/3844.htm.

[18] Strong, James. "2564 καλέω (kal-eh'-o)," Strong's Greek: 2564. καλέω (kal-eh'-o) (BibleHub, 2023), https://biblehub.com/greek/strongs/2564.htm.

He will be in us; He will make His home in us. The apostle Paul affirms this great truth in First Corinthians 6:19 where he says, "Do you not know that your body is the temple of the Holy Spirit who is in you?" When Jesus ascended back to heaven to sit at the right hand of the Father, He prayed the Father, and the Father sent another Advocate, the Holy Spirit, from heaven's home to our home.

When you look at the word for another, it is the Greek word allos, which means, "other or another of the same kind."[19] When the Lord Jesus said that He would send us another Comforter, He was referring to the third Person of the Trinity, the Holy Spirit. So, He was saying that the Holy Spirit would be One besides Him and in addition to Him, but One just like Him, of the same kind and of the same nature. I believe that is why the Lord Jesus says of the Holy Spirit in John 15:26 that "He will testify of Me," and again, in John 16:13–14, "He will not speak on His own authority, but whatever He hears He will speak… He will glorify Me, for He will take of what is Mine and declare it to you." One of a different kind, heteros,[20] would not do so. There is perfect unity in the Trinity, the Tri-une God—Father, Son, and Holy Spirit. The Son only says what He hears the Father saying, and the Holy Spirit only speaks what He hears the Son speaking. They are truly

---

[19] Strong, James. "243 ἄλλος (al'-los)," Strong's Greek: 243. ἄλλος (al'-los) (BibleHub, 2023), https://biblehub.com/greek/strongs/243.htm.
[20] Strong, James. "2087 ἕτερος (het'-er-os)," Strong's Greek: 2087. ἕτερος (het'-er-os) (BibleHub, 2023), https://biblehub.com/greek/strongs/2087.htm.

allos—distinct from one another, but just like one another, of the same nature, the same Spirit.

We have sometimes heard from those who quote Isaiah 42:8, that God will not share His glory with another, meaning that we have no right to share in His glory. However, when you look at the Hebrew word for another in this Scripture, it means "one of another kind."[21] When we surrender our lives to the Lord Jesus, we become one with Him; we join ourselves to Him, much like a man and woman who marry join themselves to one another and become one. The Bible speaks of believers being the "Bride of Christ," and Jesus being the "Bridegroom." Romans 8:29 says that we are predestined to become like Him, the same kind as Him, coming back to what God originally intended, to be made in His image and likeness.

When God created the man and then took a side of the man and created the woman, they reflected the glory of God. By creating them, God shared His glory with them. However, when they disobeyed His command to not eat from the tree of the knowledge of good and evil, through the deception of the serpent, Satan, they became another kind. They became a different kind, a slave to the kind that deceived them, and the glory of God departed from them.

The Lord Jesus declares several times in John 17 that the glory the Father gave to Him, He has shared with us. We were meant to be partakers of His glory, that He might be

---

[21] Strong, James. "312 אַחֵר (akh-air')," Strong's Hebrew: 312 אַחֵר (akh-air') (BibleHub, 2023), https://biblehub.com/hebrew/312.htm.

glorified on the earth, in and through us. Second Peter 1:4 says that through the knowledge of our Advocate, the Lord Jesus, we might be partakers of the divine nature with the accompanying glory.

However, there is still an adversary with whom we must contend. In Matthew 3:16–17, we see the Lord Jesus coming up out of the waters of baptism, and He sees the heavens opened, and the Holy Spirit descending upon Him, and the voice of the Father in heaven declaring that this Jesus was His beloved Son. He was an amazing display of the glory of God. Now this glory, and this beloved Son, Jesus, would be challenged, tested, and proven to be whom the Father declared Him to be.

Soon after His glorious baptism, the Spirit led Jesus (or drove Him, as the gospel of Mark says) into a not-so-glorious wilderness to be tempted by the devil. We may often find after a glorious experience with our Advocate, a not-so-glorious experience with our adversary. I believe this is a model for understanding the working of our Advocate in relation to our adversary. It was not the adversary who took the initiative; it was not the adversary who had free reign to do as he pleased. It was the Advocate who took the initiative to do as He pleased! The Spirit drove the Lord Jesus into the wilderness. The Spirit (Advocate) **permitted** the adversary to tempt the Lord Jesus for forty days. Again, not to do as the adversary pleased, but to do as the Advocate pleased. Our Advocate knows every step of our adversary, and He is **always** one step ahead of him. He knows every plan of every man (and woman) and has already planned for it to conform to **His** plan. If it doesn't, it won't be permitted.

Our heavenly Father was determined to prove that this was His beloved Son, in whom He was well pleased (Mt. 3:17). Therefore, the Son had to be put to the test to prove it, just as the first Adam was put to the test and failed. This Adam would not fail, and that is why He is referred to as the "last Adam." There would never be a need for another Adam. This Adam would restore to mankind everything the first Adam lost in the garden. Of course, for now we still live in a troubled world, but this will eventually give way to a new untroubled world. In the meantime, we don't have to be troubled by this world. The Lord Jesus, our Advocate, says in John 14:1, "Let not your heart be troubled; you believe in God, believe also in Me."

The adversary tempted the Lord Jesus, trying to bring Him under his power and prove His failure. However, the Advocate was testing Him to prove that He was who He said He was.

Our adversary is a tempter (Matt. 4:3); our Advocate is a tester. The Advocate is also our Helper in our weakness, to give us the fortitude to pass the test. We must prove that we are who we say we are. Declaration must be proven by demonstration. Our declaration is only as good as our demonstration. It has been said that "actions speak louder than words." Romans 5:8 says that God **demonstrated** His love for us while we were still sinners by sending His only begotten Son to die for us. Our Advocate declared it, and then He proved it. That is why we can trust the Word of God—it is a proven word.

The Lord Jesus is about to demonstrate that He is who the Father said He was. He does not resist being driven into the wilderness. There is no record of Him complaining about having to endure the tempting of the adversary. He fasted for forty days and forty nights. Where did He sleep? What did He do all that time in the wilderness? How could this be happening to the Son of God? Among other reasons, God allowed this to be an example for us, to let us know that if it happened to Him, it will happen to us. He says in John 15:20, "If they persecuted Me, they will also persecute you."

The Lord Jesus is the Captain of our salvation, the supreme example of a life that is well-pleasing to God, demonstrated in every circumstance so that we would know that whatever comes our way came His way first. He loved us first and demonstrated that love on the cross. His love was the greatest demonstration and verification that He was, and is, and ever more shall be the glorious Son of God, as the Roman centurion who helped carry out His crucifixion declared, "Truly this was the Son of God." He didn't just hear it, he "saw" it. If the world around us is going to see Christ in us, there will have to be more than declaration; there will have to be a demonstration, often at the hands of our adversary who is out to disprove what our Advocate is out to prove—that we are truly sons and daughters of God, come what may.

At the end of forty days and nights of fasting, our Advocate is now supremely tested by His adversary. "If You are the Son of God, command that these stones become bread" (Matt. 4:3). Our adversary has not changed his strategy of trying to get us to take matters into our own hands and out of our Advocate's hands, just as he did with the first woman and man. This is exactly how the Lord Jesus is being tempted. If we really think about it, this was no small temptation. The Lord Jesus is now in the fortieth day of fasting. It is known that at this point in fasting hunger returns with an intensity that is a matter of life and death. The body is beginning to break down the proteins and feed upon itself. Jesus is headed toward death if He doesn't eat soon. He had the power to turn the stones into bread, but if He did, He would betray His dependence upon and commitment to the will of the Father, saving Himself and none of the rest of us. The Father didn't send Him to save Himself, but to give Himself completely over to the will of the Father, not the will of the adversary. In John 6:38, Jesus declares, "For I have come down from heaven, not to do My own will, but the will of Him who sent Me."

And so, He responds to the adversary, "It is written..." that portion of the written Word of God that becomes the spoken, living Word of God to counter the verbal attack of the adversary (Matt. 4:4). Again, our supreme example demonstrates for us how to meet the temptation of the adversary and not take matters into our own hands. We must know the written Word of God, and the Holy Spirit will bring it to our remembrance as a living Word in our time of temptation. Jesus said He would do this in John 14:26, "He will…bring to your remembrance all things that I said to you."

The Lord Jesus finishes His response to the temptation to turn stones into bread by quoting Deuteronomy, "Man shall not live by bread alone, but by every word that proceeds from the mouth of God" (Matt. 4:4) This is how we live; this is how we think; this is how we look at things; this is how we make our decisions. Our Advocate has a word for every situation.

What we see here is the primary strategy our adversary uses to attempt to take us down. The tiny little word if tempts us to take matters into our own hands. If you're a child of God, throw away your medication, don't go to a doctor. That is not the voice of our Advocate. The voice of our Advocate does not say, "If we are His child." He says, "You **are** My child." We don't do the proving. He does the proving. I know of a person years ago who was diagnosed early with a particular form of cancer. They could have received early treatments and their life been spared. However, this person was strongly persuaded that they were a child of God and He would take care of them. They decided to follow that advice until it was too late. We dare not give in to the temptation to take matters into our own hands to prove we are a child of God. We prove we are His child by living by every word that **He** speaks to us and confirms in the mouths of two and three witnesses (2 Cor. 13:1), not by the word of our adversary. We know that he can masquerade as an angel of light to deceive us with darkness (2 Cor. 11:14).

Our adversary can also use that tiny little word if to tempt us to doubt the integrity of our Advocate. If God is such a loving God, why does He let bad things happen to people? Why doesn't He heal everybody who needs healing? Why am I going through this awful situation with my family? Why would He send anybody to hell? How do you know you can trust Him? And as the serpent said to Eve in the garden, "Did God **really** say…?"

Following the death of our son, people asked us, "Aren't you angry with God for taking your first-born son? Aren't you angry with God that you didn't get to see him live out his dream of becoming a judge, getting married, having children?" These are real questions and emotions we can grapple with. We don't have to hide them or deny them; we can pour out our complaint to our Advocate. We must never let our adversary use it to incite us to complain against our Advocate. We dare not fall prey to the temptation to blame God as though He did us wrong. If He did something wrong, then He can't be God. If He isn't perfect in all His ways, then He can't be trusted and we can't be comforted.

Having to part with a child, and in our case with a first-born child, is out of the natural order of things. It is difficult. Having to do it without the help of our Helper, our Advocate, because I'm blaming Him and angry with Him, is unimaginable. We are reminded of the fact that we dedicated that son as an infant to God who gave him, acknowledging that he was first and foremost His son before he was ours. He gave him to us for a season, however long or short the season, to bring him to the knowledge of the One to whom he rightfully belonged.

With respect to our Advocate "taking" our son from us, the Lord reminded me one day that He enlightened both my wife and me independently, without each other's knowledge, one hour before his departure, that we were to surrender him to the will of God. He gave us the grace to do that. We didn't do it "kicking and screaming." We knew that it was the will of God. Our son was fighting to stay alive, not for his sake, but for our sake. He was ready to go—he had seen the face of Jesus! We could not demand that he stay here with us, when he could be there with Him, which is the blessed hope of all who put their faith in the risen Christ. Even though we still miss him dearly, we are also envious of the fact that he got there ahead of us.

So, our Advocate didn't **take** him, He waited for us to **give** him over to his rightful Parent. The Lord Jesus said that no one could take His life from Him, He willingly gave it (John 10:18). He didn't go to the cross "kicking and screaming." He settled that in the garden of Gethsemane. He was like a Lamb led to the slaughter and He didn't open His mouth (to protest) (Isa. 53:7).

The last question I believe the Lord clarified for us had to do with our son's statement that one day he would become a judge. I was driving home in my car one day, not really thinking about anything, when out of nowhere the Scripture came to me, "Do you not know that the saints will judge the world?" (1 Cor. 6:2). I suddenly realized then that our son would, after all, be a judge, not here, but on the new earth, in the city of the "New Jerusalem." I believe that whatever we don't get to finish here, we will finish there, forever!

And so, the adversary continues his quest to tempt our Advocate to sin, and our Advocate is willing to endure it for our sakes to reverse the failure of the first Adam that brought the curse of sin into the world. He is a true Advocate. He is for us, as Romans 8:31 says.

The adversary takes the Lord Jesus into the Holy City and sets Him on the pinnacle of the temple (Matt. 4:5). The Lord Jesus lets him do it, whereas, He could have snuffed him out right then and there. However, because our Advocate was totally committed to the will and plan of the Father, to stand in our place in every way, He submitted Himself. At this point, the adversary tempts the Lord Jesus to throw Himself down to prove that He's the Son of God, and even quotes Scripture to support it. Setting Him on the highest point of the temple, which was the most holy place of the Jews, would suggest that He was above all and nothing could hurt Him. Our Advocate responds with the Scripture that is in line with His submission to the will of the Father, "You shall not tempt [or put to the test] the Lord your God" (Matt. 4:7). The adversary was manipulating the Scriptures with his own will to tempt the Lord Jesus to sin. The adversary will always use the Scriptures, if he knows we know them, to appeal to our own fleshly will.

We must never succumb to the temptation to use the Scriptures according to our own agenda or to get what we want. There is a way that seems right to the natural man or woman, but in the end, it leads to destruction, just as it did for the first man and woman (Prov. 14:12). Second Timothy 3:16 says, "All Scripture is given by inspiration of God, and is profitable for doctrine, for reproof, for correction, for instruction in righteousness." We see that it is intended for use according to God's purposes, not according to our purposes. We must have the same inspiration in our use of the Scriptures—the inspiration of the Holy Spirit.

The Lord Jesus, our Advocate, is our supreme example in the garden of Gethsemane. He declares a scriptural truth in Mark 14:36, when He says, "Father, all things are possible for You. Take this cup away from Me." There is nothing our Advocate can't do. There is no way He can't make. He could have made another way for the Lord Jesus, and the Lord Jesus could have continued to claim that scriptural truth, but after agonizing before the Father, it comes down to the **will** of the Father over the **ability** of the Father. Isaiah 30:20–21 says, "And though the Lord gives you the bread of adversity and the water of affliction…your ears shall hear a word behind you saying, 'This is the way, walk in it.'" At times, our Advocate chooses a way for us that we would not choose, but it is during those agonizing times that we must trust that His way is the best way, and we will end up seeing it. There are many things that our Advocate can do that He does not do. There are many things He can prevent that He does not prevent. His will is supreme and is the best course of action. The Lord Jesus came to fulfill the Scriptures, one of which says that He would be a Lamb led to the slaughter (Isa. 53:7). He was willing to become one of us. He had to wrestle with the same things we wrestle with in order to be our great High Priest who is touched with our feelings (Heb. 4:15). And so, the Lord Jesus, our Advocate, exclaims, "Nevertheless [despite the fact that all things are possible with You], not what I will, but what You will" (Mark 14:36).

As we said before, God doesn't always do what He is able to do, but He always does what He wills to do. When Lazarus was sick and dying, they came to the Lord Jesus to do what He was able to do, expecting Him to come immediately and heal him, but the Lord Jesus stayed where He was for two more days, and Lazarus died. How could that be? Why wouldn't the Lord Jesus come and do what He was able to do? Lazarus's sisters and all the people wondered the same thing. "Lord, if You had just been here, he wouldn't have died," they said. The Lord Jesus had said to His disciples that Lazarus's sickness was "not unto death" (John 11:4). However, Lazarus died. The Lord Jesus was saying that death was not going to be the end. It may look that way, but it's not going to end that way. But this did not mean that He would heal Lazarus, even though He could have healed him. He would raise Lazarus from the dead to demonstrate the power of His resurrection and the fact that He was the resurrection and the life for all humanity.

When our Advocate doesn't do what He's able to do in any given situation, it is only because He intends to do something else. He is able to heal and to raise from the dead. He decides which course of action He's going to take according to His will. We can be assured that He hears us, and He will answer.

In Matthew 8:2, a leper came to the Lord Jesus and worshipped Him, which would indicate that God revealed to him that this was the Son of God. The verse records the leper saying, "Lord, if You are willing, You can make me clean." He didn't say, "If You are able." He had already addressed Him as "Lord," and believed He was able. He humbled himself under His Lordship, rather than assuming that because He was the Lord and was able to make him clean, He should do it. He said to the Lord Jesus, "If You are **willing**." In other words, it's all up to You. It is my will to be cleansed from this leprosy, but I subordinate my will to Yours.

There may be some who take the position that it is always God's will to heal, to deliver, to change the natural or physical circumstances of a situation. While I believe that is generally true, we must take into consideration the season in which God is working. We can't put God in a box and say that He always does it a certain way, or the Word says this or that, so it must be so. God is not bound by the Word that I choose to stand on, but He is bound by **His** Word, the Word of **His** choosing that comes from **His** mouth. Our Advocate will never be put in a box and brought down to our level. Isaiah 55:9 says that His ways are higher than our ways, and His thoughts are higher than our thoughts. As mentioned earlier, Proverbs 14:12 says, "There is a way that seems right to a man, but its end is the way of death." It is not in agreement with the will of the Giver of Life.

In the case of the apostle Paul in the second letter to the Corinthians, Chapter 12, he had a "thorn in the flesh…a messenger of Satan to buffet me" (v. 7). Paul pleaded with the Lord three times that it might be taken from him. This was not the will of God. His will at that time was to keep Paul from being exalted above measure because of the abundance of revelations given to him and the manifestations of the glory of God working through him in signs, wonders, and miracles. It wasn't the time for **healing**, it was the time for **humbling**. The apostle Paul could have quoted Old and New Testament Scriptures of God his healer and deliverer. We can quote those Scriptures all we dare to, but if that is not in agreement with His will and purpose for that particular time, it shall not come to pass. We must be willing to receive and live by every Word that comes out of the mouth of God (the spoken word, Rhema,[22] from the written word, Logos[23]), not just the word supporting our position or desire.

---

[22] Strong, James. "4487 ῥῆμα (hray'-mah)," Strong's Greek: 4487. ῥῆμα (hray'-mah) (BibleHub, 2023), https://biblehub.com/greek/strongs/4487.htm.
[23] Strong, James. "3056 λόγος (log'-os)," Strong's Greek: 3056. λόγος (log'-os) (BibleHub, 2023), https://biblehub.com/greek/strongs/3056.htm.

After Paul's impassioned triple plea unto the Lord, Second Corinthians 12:9 tells us God's response (the Rhema out of the Logos), "And He said to me, 'My grace is sufficient for you.'" The Scriptures are not only written about healing, they are also written about grace. Our Advocate did not heal Paul, but He gave him a sufficient measure of grace to carry him through the pain. A measure of grace that will sustain him, while at the same time causing him to know that the strength of His Advocate is made perfect in his weakness. Isaiah 40:29 says, "He gives power to the weak, and to those who have no might He increases strength." He is saying to Paul, "Through your weakness, caused by the thorn in your flesh, will come supernatural strength. I will strengthen you in the midst of your pain and keep you from being exalted above measure." Even though it is the work of the adversary against the apostle Paul, the greater work of the Advocate keeps His servant from the destruction of pride. Some of us are inclined to get puffed up with pride when God shows up and manifests His glory through us. Our Advocate is faithful. We can count on Him to keep us from falling prey to pride by whatever means He chooses to prevent it, even if it is at the hand of our adversary.

As we go back to the temptation of our Advocate by our adversary, we see that the adversary attempts to advance his agenda of deception with the written Scriptures (logos), but our Advocate counters them with the Father's agenda to meet and defeat each one with the spoken word (rhema) from above.

> *But if you have bitter envy and self-seeking in your hearts, do not boast and lie against the truth. This wisdom does not descend from above, but is earthly, sensual, demonic.*
>
> (James 3:14–15)

James goes on to say,

> *"But the wisdom that is from above is first pure, then peaceable, gentle, willing to yield, full of mercy and good fruits, without partiality and without hypocrisy"*
>
> (v. 17).

The adversary's use of the Scriptures does not come from above; it comes from below. It is from bitter envy, self-seeking, and every evil thing that exalts itself above the knowledge of God. It is earthly, sensual, and demonic in origin. It is the polar opposite of the wisdom from above which is pure and peaceable. The wisdom from above is **willing to yield** and give the right of way to God. Our adversary is unwilling to yield. He wants to take the place of God in our lives in any way he can. First Samuel 15:23 compares rebellion to the sin of witchcraft. The spirit of witchcraft is a controlling spirit—a desire to be in control and have control over others. The Lord Jesus will never seek to control us. He doesn't have to. He is Lord of lords and Lord over all. He seeks not to control, but to convince us of the truth to win us over. I like to say, "God didn't run me over, He won me over." He will never violate our will. This is in stark contrast to our adversary's attempt to control us with fear and intimidation.

The adversary can do no more. The Lord Jesus will not yield to his deceptive temptations. Luke 4:13 says, "Now when the devil had ended **every** temptation," suggesting that there may have been many more than three. It is possible that there were three categories of temptations with multiple temptations in each category. Mark's gospel states that our Advocate was tempted in the wilderness by Satan forty days and nights and was with the wild beasts. The adversary pulled everything out of his arsenal to take down our Advocate, but he could not succeed. And so, he departed from Him until he had another opportunity. He would be back for another round, and this one would be the final round.

Luke chapter 22 relates how the adversary returns as the Lord Jesus is coming to His final hour after three years of preaching, teaching, and demonstrating the nature and life of the Kingdom of God. The opportunity has now come for the adversary to incite the chief priests and scribes to kill the Lord Jesus, and they sought how they might accomplish it. They didn't have to seek too long, because the adversary had another willing party at his disposal: Judas Iscariot. Judas was part of the inner circle of disciples, but he had a weakness. The adversary knows our weaknesses and seeks to prey upon them to accomplish his purposes. He preyed upon the jealousy of the priests and scribes, and he preyed upon Judas's love of money.

However, this was no surprise to the Lord Jesus. He says in all four gospels, and specifically in John 6:70, "Did I not choose you, the twelve, and one of you is a devil?" He was speaking of Judas Iscariot. Why would the Lord Jesus choose a devil as one of His disciples? Didn't He know what He was doing? He knew exactly what He was doing, because He knew the Father, and He knew the Scriptures, and He came to fulfill all the will of the Father, and all that was written, despite what it might mean for Him. He didn't come for His own comfort; He came for our comfort. Psalm 41:9 says of the Lord Jesus, "Even my own familiar friend in whom I trusted, who ate my bread, has lifted up his heel against [betrayed] me." Again, this is the main point of this book; we have an Advocate with the Father. We need one, not only to plead our case for the remission of sin, but because we have an adversary who seeks to devour us (1 Pet. 5:8).

Our adversary would like nothing more than to devour and extinguish our faith in the Lord Jesus by whatever means he is permitted, just as he incited Judas to betray Him to the Jewish religious leaders who sought to extinguish Him so that no one could have faith in Him. The primary goal of our adversary is to erode and eradicate our faith in the Lord Jesus.

Further on, in Luke 22:31–32, the Lord Jesus lets Peter know that "Satan has asked for you, that he may sift you as wheat. But I have prayed for you, that your faith should not fail; and when you have returned to Me, strengthen your brethren." They, too, will abandon Him. Peter responds by saying that he was ready to go to prison with the Lord Jesus, and even die with Him. The Lord Jesus knew better. He knows the weakness of human flesh. The spirit is willing, but the flesh is weak (Matt. 26:41), and that is the area the adversary targets to bring us down. The Lord predicted that Peter would deny that He ever knew the Lord Jesus, not once, but three times, the third time with cursing. Peter's faith in the Lord Jesus faltered through the weakness of his flesh, but it was resurrected through the power of the Spirit on the day of Pentecost. The Holy Spirit was poured out on him and 119 others in an upper room behind closed doors like a mighty rushing wind and filled them all with power and boldness to witness for the Lord Jesus. This was led by none other than Peter, himself, and three thousand souls believed on the Lord Jesus and were added to their number in one day. Hallelujah!

The adversary has employed the willing parties of the Jewish religious leaders, and Judas, the traitor, to deliver what they thought would be the final blow to bring down the Lord Jesus. When we are suffering adversity at the hand of our adversary, he will never deliver the final blow. The final blow has already been delivered to him by Jesus's death on the cross. If the Jewish religious leaders had known that they would only be part of our Advocate's predetermined plan to save the world, they would have never done it. And neither would the adversary. But they were all blinded by their murderous jealousy of the Lord Jesus, and there was no turning back. They shouted, "Crucify Him, Crucify Him," even when Pilate found no cause for it and wanted to let Him go.

Acts 4:27–28 tells us that God had determined beforehand that all of this would happen, that Herod and Pontius Pilate and the Jewish leaders would be His tools. Our Advocate knows every plan of our adversary from beginning to end because He is the Beginning and the End, the First and the Last, the Alpha and the Omega (Rev. 22:13). He started it all, and He will end it all. Our Advocate had the first word, and He will have the last word, conforming all things to His will, not the will of our adversary (Eph. 1:11). The Lord Jesus knew this. He knew the Scriptures, and He knew the will of the Father. He told His disciples beforehand what would occur. It is crucial for us to know every word of the Scriptures and to know the Father with such intimacy as to know His will at any given time, in any given situation, and to be able to rest in the hope of salvation, the hope of resurrection, and the hope of the glory to come.

Hope does not come without a Gethsemane. We still have to deal with our flesh. Remember, the spirit is willing, but the flesh susceptible to the strategies of our adversary. The Lord Jesus isn't facing a walk in the park. He is facing all the powers of darkness coming against Him. He said to the chief priests and elders who came to apprehend Him, "This is your hour, and the power of darkness" (Luke 22:53).

Matthew 26:37 says that the Lord Jesus took Peter, James, and John into the garden of Gethsemane with Him, and He began to be filled with sorrow and distress, just as it was prophesied of Him in Isaiah 53:3–4. In Matthew 26:38, Jesus says, "My soul is exceedingly sorrowful, even unto death." He is experiencing for us the sorrow of death caused by sin. The prospect of what He is facing is agonizing for Him to the point of falling on His face before the Father, and asking Him to take the cup from Him. Mark's gospel puts it in even stronger terms in Chapter 14:36: "Abba (Daddy), Father, all things are possible for You. Take this cup away from Me." The Lord Jesus was not only the Son of God, He was also the Son of Man, meaning that He was fully God and fully human. He left His glory in heaven to become a man, to share in our humanity and become one of us. He fully identified with us in our humanity. He was willing to be tempted and tried in every way we would ever be, but without sin so that He could be our qualified sacrifice for our sin.

A sinner cannot take the place of another sinner any more than a prisoner on death row could take the place of another prisoner on death row—they are both under the same condemnation. Only the innocent can take the place of the guilty for exoneration of the guilty, and that is exactly what the Lord Jesus came to do. He could not bypass His humanity on the way to the cross. He would not be forced to suffer against His will. He would have to become willing to suffer if that was the will of the Father. There had to be a Gethsemane before there was a cross. His will was put to the supreme test as the supreme example for all humanity.

Adam and Eve had failed the test and brought death to all humanity and to all that God had created.

Three times the Lord Jesus agonizes before the Father, sweating with such intensity that His blood vessels burst and turned His drops of sweat into drops of blood (Luke 22:44). He was already bleeding before He even got to the cross! The matter is already being settled in the garden by our great Advocate. Each time He appeals to the Father, He ends up saying, "Not My will, but Your will be done." This was the issue to be settled. It is not so much a matter of what we go through; it is what we are **willing** to go through if it is the will of the Father. He is the Chief Executive of the Godhead, but He will never impose His will on us. He didn't make us that way; He didn't want us that way. He wanted us to love Him as He loved us, willingly enough to embrace His will come what may. To trust Him enough to believe that whatever His will is will result in life, even bringing life out of death.

Our Advocate, the Lord Jesus, says in John 10:18, "No one takes it [My life] from Me, but I lay it down of Myself. I have power to lay it down, and I have power to take it again." God made us with the power to lay down our lives. He gave us the power to choose. We are the only kind of His creation with such power, and we live and die by the choices we make. Adam and Eve made one choice that brought death into all of God's creation, and all of humanity. Romans 5:19 says, "For as by one man's disobedience many were made sinners [and subject to eternal death], so also by one Man's obedience many will be made righteous [and gain eternal life]."

Our Advocate made the choice in the garden of Gethsemane to surrender to the will of the Father, which meant death for Him, but life for us. The choice He made in the garden led to the cross. Our Advocate has taken the keys of death and hell from our adversary. He can no longer keep us locked up as prisoners to sin and unrighteousness. We are now, "prisoners" of the Lord to do His will and walk in paths of righteousness. To be free to be a servant of the Lord is true freedom. Freedom is not being able to do as I please; that is slavery to my appetites, my lusts, my greed—all of which lead to death just as they did for the first man and woman. John 8:36 tells us that if Jesus sets us free, we are truly free. Galatians 5:1 says, "Stand fast therefore in the liberty by which Christ has made us free, and do not be entangled again with a yoke of bondage." We no longer need to choose sin. The Holy Spirit lives in us and empowers us with the freedom to choose life and righteousness. Where the Spirit of the Lord is, there is freedom (2 Cor. 3:17) and where is the Spirit of the Lord? In us. Philippians 2:13 says that it is God (the Holy Spirit) who works in us both to have the will (choice) and to do what pleases Him. Romans 8:11 says, "If the Spirit of Him who raised Jesus from the dead dwells in you, He who raised Christ from the dead will also give life to your mortal bodies through His Spirit who dwells in you." There is no other way it can happen. Left to ourselves, we are doomed to make choices for death even when we want to make choices for life.

The apostle Paul makes reference to this in Romans chapter seven. "For what I am doing, I do not understand. For what I will to do, that I do not practice; but what I hate, that I do" (v. 15). This hearkens all the way back to the beginning after God created the man and then created the woman out of the man, and made a garden for them to live in with Him. He provided everything they would ever need and gave them permission to eat from any tree of the garden, except one—the tree of the knowledge of good and evil. Evil will always be there when you want to do good. The adversary will have the upper hand, and this is Paul's lament until he finally cries out in verses 24 and 25, "O wretched man that I am! Who will deliver me from this body of death? I thank God—through Jesus Christ our Lord!"

He has and He will.

Our Advocate is our Deliverer. He delivers us from the hand of our adversary, setting us free from the power of sin and supplanting it with the power of the Holy Spirit. We must understand that as long as we live in this flesh, our adversary will continue his efforts to intimidate us and take us down. There may be intimidation, but there will not be occupation by our adversary as long as we are covered by the blood of our Advocate, the Lamb of God, and take our stand upon the victory of His cross. We are safe with Him. Greater is He who is in us than the one who is in the world and stands against us (1 John 4:4). Thanks be to God through our Lord Jesus Christ!

About the Author

Pastor Jack Rehill is an ordained minister with the Assemblies of God. He earned his Bachelor of Arts in Sociology from Kings College and his Masters of Social Work from Marywood University. He also participated in a post-graduate program in Structural Family Therapy through Philadelphia Child Guidance and is certified as a Structural Family Therapist.

He has served as President/CEO of the local subsidiary of the Volunteers of America Christian Social Service Agency, serving children, teens, and adults in various therapeutic settings. As a PA-licensed clinical social worker, Jack has worked in the mental health field & Christ-directed counseling for over 42 years.

When first saved, coming out of the "hippie" generation of the sixties, Jack desired to go straight into Bible College and ministry. However, the Lord very clearly told him to "stay in his course of study, and He would use me in that field." Many years later, after accepting a position with Volunteers of America, he became a licensed minister. He says, "The Lord showed me that my desire to move into ministry from many years ago was happening."

Outside of his love for ministry, Jack is an avid exercise enthusiast: from racquetball to basketball to weightlifting. Once in a while, he enjoys driving a Sprint Cup race car at Pocono Raceway at speeds of 150 mph.

Jack and his wife Patti were married in August of 1971. They have four children & two granddaughters. Patti has been an Administrative Assistant at Harvest Church for nearly 20 years. Before Harvest, she earned her degree in nursing and worked in a variety of settings, from hospitals to home health.

Jack and Patti are beach lovers and try to get there as often as scheduling permits. They enjoy worship music, both contemporary and some of the old favorites from years past.

Patti loves to cook and bake, so they also love hosting people in our home to share a meal (and perhaps a game or two of Catch Phrase)!

Watch for Jack Rehill's next book:

The Mediator

Made in the USA
Columbia, SC
09 June 2025